AND CHEER FOR THE GREEN AND GOLD

AND CHEER FOR THE GREEN AND GOLD

An Anecdotal History of The Chapin School

Charlotte Johnson Noerdlinger

THE CHAPIN SCHOOL

CONTENTS

INTRODUCTION
·—·
7

CHAPTER ONE
·—·
*The Early
Years*
·—·
11

CHAPTER TWO
·—·
Traditions

31

CHAPTER THREE
·—·
Time for Change

59

CHAPTER FOUR

The Stringfellow Years

79

CHAPTER FIVE

*The
Wheel Turns*

105

CHAPTER SIX

*Preparing
for a New
Century*

141

FROM THE AUTHOR 151 · ACKNOWLEDGMENTS 151 · APPENDIX 152 · INDEX 158

INTRODUCTION

*It is given to very few to realize their dreams, to see an
ideal come into being in greater perfection than one had
thought possible.*

Mrs. Harold I. Pratt
President of the Board of Trustees, 1927–1929

Maria Bowen Chapin founded Miss Chapin's School for Girls and
Kindergarten for Boys and Girls in 1901, the year that Theodore Roosevelt
became president of the United States. Although the president and Miss
Chapin probably never met, they were certainly kindred spirits. Both
were inspired leaders with a mission—Mr. Roosevelt's for leading his
country, Miss Chapin's for educating young women. Both put morality
first, before health, worldly success, or academic achievement, and both
fervently believed that God was on their side. Miss Chapin's abiding
faith in God was reflected in all she said and did. Her strength sprang
from the absolute certainty of her belief in God, in the value of honor
and honesty, and in the obligation to help one's fellow man.

Miss Chapin's personal calling was to the education of young women,
particularly the daughters of New York's leading families. She was
keenly aware that her students would grow up not only to run homes,
but also to serve on charitable committees and boards. For her day, she
was an ardent feminist. She believed that women were capable of doing
anything they wanted to do, and that they merited the same rigorous

The School Song

7

classical education that their brothers received, rather than the traditional Victorian girls' curriculum of music, art, needlepoint and French. She thought that if they were to grow to be wise women, they had to learn history, literature, science, Latin and Greek. Moreover, she wanted them to be able to think and speak for themselves, and at the same time to conduct themselves with dignity, prudence and good manners.

Miss Chapin threw herself into this mission not only with passion and integrity, but also with another quality that is harder to define: inspirational leadership. Joanna Bailie Gunderson '49 wrote that her

Portrait of Maria Bowen Chapin by Ellen Emmett Rand, circa 1928

After Commencement, 1960, Marion Eaton · Field Day, Marion Eaton

mother, Margaret Henderson Bailie '13, Miss Chapin's goddaughter and one of her early students, "always spoke of Miss Chapin with the greatest love. She said she reminded her of the verses from St. Paul's Epistle to the Philippians: 'Whatsoever things are true, whatsoever things are honest, whatsoever things are just, whatsoever things are pure, whatsoever things are lovely, whatsoever things are of good report; if there be any virtue, and if there be any praise, think on these things.'" Indeed, love, for her, and for everything she stood for, was an emotion shared by nearly everyone who knew her. Margaret Henderson Bailie herself wrote, "To me Miss Chapin has always seemed to personify all St. Paul's whatsoevers, with the added whatsoever things were kind, gay and comforting and whatsoever things were fun."

Generations of young women have benefited from Miss Chapin's decision to found a school. Even today, her spirit permeates the school's halls and classrooms, and guides its policies. Miss Chapin's colleagues and successors—Miss Fairfax, Miss Stringfellow, Mrs. Berendsen, and now, Ms. Theunick—have all been faithful to the founder's spirit, carrying on the values and traditions that she personified, and adapting them to the enormous changes of the twentieth century. Under their direction, the Chapin School has flourished. What follows here is an anecdotal account of how the school began, the challenges it overcame and how it prospered.

CHAPTER ONE

THE EARLY YEARS

She personally represented all that was best and most beautiful and most indestructible. She was the epitome of a great educator.

ALETHIA SHELDON '32, ON MISS CHAPIN

Very little is known about Maria Bowen Chapin's early years. She was born on September 13, 1863, in Wickford, Rhode Island, one of seven children—four sons and three daughters. Her father, Walter Bartlett Chapin, a manufacturer and broker, was descended from Deacon Samuel Chapin, who had come to America in the early seventeenth century to become one of the founders of Springfield, Massachusetts. Her mother, Frances Viall, was descended from William Viall, who settled at Seekonk, Rhode Island, about 1790.

The Chapin family traveled extensively. Maria was thus generally tutored, both at home and abroad. Her one year at school was spent at Miss Abbott's School in Providence, Rhode Island, when she was a teenager. This school had a profound effect on her; she would later adopt many of its traditions in the school she herself was to found.

Unfortunately, Walter Chapin, having made his fortune in shipping, suffered severe financial reversals. One day he unexpectedly announced to his family that they had become quite poor. There would be no further opportunities for education and travel. To make matters

Maria Bowen Chapin, circa 1888

Maria Bowen Chapin
as a child

more difficult, Frances Chapin had become an invalid, and Maria had little choice but to stay at home and take care of her mother and the household. She tutored some of her brothers' classmates at a neighborhood boys' school. Some poems written during these years underscore both personal anguish and religious faith.

In 1888, after her mother's death, Maria was persuaded by her close friend Helen Iselin to come to New York to be a teacher, one of the few employment opportunities open to an educated young woman. At this time, not many private schools admitted pupils under the age of ten. Younger children were instead taught at home by privately hired teachers. Well-to-do families joined together to support these tutorials until their children were old enough to enter the leading private schools—Brearley and Spence for girls, and Browning and Allen-Stevenson for boys. Public schools were not considered suitable for a child from a socially prominent family.

Miss Chapin's first pupils in New York were six little girls whom she taught in the parlor of Mrs. John Atterbury. She later wrote, "I tried to teach for money because I wished to earn my living.… I began without training…and I am glad I was given a chance to learn by practice, though it makes me feel very uncomfortable when I realize how much my training must have cost the innocent pupils who gave it to me. For two years I taught such private pupils as I could persuade into my net—all small and of unduly confiding parentage." Since this particular group of girls was destined for the Brearley School, Miss Chapin kept in close touch with James G. Croswell, headmaster of the school, and his secretary, Alice Wetmore. Miss Wetmore, like Miss Chapin, was from Providence, where she had attended the Kindergarten Training School. The two ladies became friends as well as colleagues, and in 1894 Miss

Life is soft music into silence dying.
The drowsy murmur of the idle bees;
The mother-robin's plaintive minor crying
The gossip winds' swift whisper in the trees.

A poetry fragment revealing Miss Chapin's romantic side

Letter of agreement from Miss Chapin to Miss Wetmore

Wetmore asked Miss Chapin to join her in starting a school. Mr. Croswell gave them his full support, as they would be preparing girls for Brearley. The combination seemed ideal: Miss Wetmore knew the mechanics of running a school, while Miss Chapin was a gifted teacher and would be able to attract the students through the wide circle of friends that she had developed in New York.

The new venture was called Primary Classes for Girls. In their agreement, Miss Wetmore was to be the administrator and sole proprietor, and Miss Chapin was "to take charge of the educational side. The teaching staff consisted of a singing teacher, a gymnasium teacher and a writing teacher in addition to my eager and inexperienced self…. We started with eighteen pupils the first year. We doubled our number the second year, and before the third, Miss Wetmore and I took a house for the growing school [at 12 East Forty-fifth Street] and became partners."

Within two years Miss Chapin's idea of establishing a "joint proprietorship" upset Miss Wetmore, who was determined to keep the school and its bank account solely in her name. "I invented Primary Classes and found most of the pupils," Miss Wetmore stormed. "I didn't start my school to have it named Miss Chapin's."

Miss Chapin was equally determined to assume more authority. Although a new agreement was not signed until the middle of December 1896, Miss Wetmore finally capitulated, agreeing to have the school's bank account issued in both their names, and to have new circulars and billheads printed acknowledging Miss Chapin's authority as equal to her own.

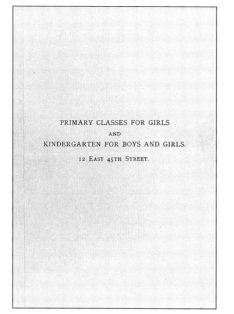

PRIMARY CLASSES FOR GIRLS
AND
KINDERGARTEN FOR BOYS AND GIRLS.
12 EAST 45TH STREET.

Conducted by Mrs. Wetmore & Miss Chap[

~~Miss Wetmore~~
~~Miss Chapin~~

These small Primary Classes are ~~under the direction of Miss Chapin, and are~~ arranged for girls from six to twelve years of age, who will be thoroughly prepared to enter more advanced classes, or Brearley School. In the Kindergarten, boys and girls, under six years of age, will be fitted for primary work.

Autumn term will begin on October 8th. Hours from 9 to 12 and 12.30, and from 10 to 12.

Tuition, $200, $250, and $275. Kindergarten, $125. The number of pupils being limited, tuition for the first half-year will be charged from the opening of school in October. No deductions are made for absence. ~~Applications and cheques for tuition should be addressed to Miss Wetmore.~~

Primary Classes Bulletin of Information

Despite their differences, the two ladies held Primary Classes for Girls together for seven years, and the school was a success. Its records show that it was expanded to include a Kindergarten for both boys and girls. With her personality, strength and vision, Miss Chapin charmed the parents and inspired her students, building toward that certain day when she would open a school of her own.

Once their new contract was signed, Miss Wetmore and Miss Chapin settled into educating the children. In the two years before 1896–1897, Miss Chapin taught most of the academic subjects herself. She must have been given free rein by Alice Wetmore, for the young teacher introduced at Primary Classes many of the features that were to become trademarks of her own school a few years later. The influence of her one year at Miss Abbott's School in Providence was marked. Josephine L. Abbott, that school's founder, herself had had a "pervading personality," and her school had been ahead of its time in curriculum and requirements. A history of the school states that "Miss Abbott had opened the school every day in the gymnasium, the teachers sitting with her on the platform; first a hymn was sung, then a prayer was offered and then a few verses were read from the Bible." In 1925 Miss Chapin wrote, "In that school we were given a standard of what a student should be."

An early alumna, Priscilla Stanton Auchincloss '06, started at Primary Classes when she was nine years old, in the autumn of 1897. "The first day I was in school Miss Chapin started us on an outline of history: 'In the old Stone Age men used stones as they found them. In the new Stone Age men sharpened and polished stones for tools and weapons.' And so on, always with equal pithiness. I can only say that this course stayed with me so well that finding an examination on 'Comprehensive History' being offered when I was taking college entrance examinations I took it on the spur of the moment—and passed." May Terry Savage, a student at Primary Classes, remembered Miss Chapin. "She gave us daily mental arithmetic speed work which she made us enjoy. Weekly News was so vivid that I remember things she said fifty-five years ago!"

In 1901 Miss Chapin and Miss Wetmore decided to end their partnership. They divided up the furniture and the fixtures, and each prepared to operate her own school.

Miss Wetmore, who was older, must have missed her energetic colleague, for in a few years she sold her school and retired.

Turning to the friend who had first encouraged her to come to New York to teach, Miss Chapin borrowed $2,000 from Helen Iselin's husband, Edward Henderson, to pay the first year's rent on a house at 12 West Forty-seventh Street, a wide thoroughfare of brownstone houses with grassy front lawns. She was able to open Miss Chapin's School for Girls and Kindergarten for Boys and Girls to seventy-eight students and seven teachers in October of 1901. From the beginning, Miss Chapin had decided that her new enterprise would be more than an elementary school. Her goal was to offer a full twelve-year program that would prepare students for college if that was their choice. James Croswell of Brearley and Clara B. Spence, headmistress of Miss Spence's School, supported her. Both "were confident there was room in New York City for another secondary school of the character they were generous enough to believe ours would become." Miss Chapin added one class each year, crowding the school but culminating in the triumphant graduation of two girls, Charlotte Harding and Sylvia Holt, in 1908.

Financial conclusion for Primary Classes

Fifth Avenue, just around the corner from 12 West Forty-seventh Street, 1906

One of the teachers at Forty-seventh Street described the first school:

On the three upper floors were the two large and two small rooms of an ordinary city house, but on the entrance floor there were three rooms, a reception room on the street, a room for the littlest children looking into the sunshine and the backyard, and a dark middle room where Miss [Julia] Wilde worked at what might be called an uncomfortable lady's desk, with a slanting lid off which papers slid more easily than they remained at rest. This was of importance, for with no automatic arrangement to ring the bells for the change of classes, Miss Wilde with her own hand had to ring the bells every half hour, which made the end of a period uncertain as all her papers might slide off her desk at the instant she was to ring the bell.

Often more than one class would be held in a room at the same time. Students had to concentrate hard not to be distracted by the different lessons being taught around them. This early training, however, proved valuable. In later years Julia Reed Palmer '33 wrote that some girls did their homework while a class was being conducted in the front of the room. "We learned to concentrate.... I can sit and write an important document in the middle of Grand Central Station."

Miss Chapin was extremely fond of the little boys she admitted to her Kindergarten, jokingly dubbing them "limbs of Satan." According to Ethel Grey Stringfellow, the school's third headmistress, Miss Chapin took young boys because there were so few schools for them in 1901. St. Bernard's was not founded until 1904 and Buckley not until 1913. One alumnus of Miss Chapin's Kindergarten recalls that the boys were always getting into trouble with her. "We played hide and seek in the locker room, tripped the girls on the concrete in the yard and hopped around during rest period, after having been inserted into bags which tied round our necks, ostensibly for warmth."

Mary Cecelia Fairfax had come to New York in 1894 to teach mathematics at Primary Classes. In 1902 she joined Miss Chapin's faculty. She had waited a year in order to honor her prior agreement with Miss Wetmore. After joining Miss Chapin, she "plunged into a career of putting the fear of God and of mathematics into succeeding generations of Chapin School girls, and of giving them a shining example of integrity, generosity and devotion, well peppered...with a lively temper."

The school offered more than an academic education. The moral development of Miss Chapin's mischievous students came first. She later wrote, "Children's morals are made up of good habits, built upon the foundation of a few fundamental principles." Her charges' health was also of paramount importance, and Miss Chapin saw to it that they had plenty of fresh air and sunshine.

Another cornerstone of the curriculum was proper elocution. Possessed of a beautiful speaking voice herself, Miss Chapin wrote, "It is speech that differentiates us from other animals, and we ought to take the greatest care with the sounds we make. Cultivation of the voice ought to take a first place in our education."

Penmanship was also of paramount importance to Miss Chapin, whose own bold and rangy script had never pleased her. She wanted her girls to perfect an elegant hand. The first teacher of penmanship, Miss Goldsmith, instructed her pupils "to keep the penholder pointed at your right ear, and then by moving your index finger and thumb, to write." A second teacher, Miss Havens, introduced a nice round script.

Music was important to Miss Chapin and, as soon as possible, she organized a choir to sing the hymns at Prayers. Mrs. Harriet Cartwright directed the choir and taught music. Her anthology *Song Treasury* was

---

Second to you 1902.03

MISS CHAPIN'S
SCHOOL FOR GIRLS
AND
KINDERGARTEN FOR BOYS AND GIRLS
12 West 47th Street

Miss Chapin's School will re-open on Wednesday, October 8th, 1902.

Classes are arranged for girls from six years of age, and pupils are prepared to enter Brearley School, or Miss Spence's School. The hours of school are from 9 to 12.30 and 1.

In connection with these classes there is a Kindergarten, in which boys and girls from three to six years of age are fitted for primary work. The Kindergarten will re-open on Monday, October 27th; hours from 9.30 to 11.30 and 12.

Tuition for the School $200, $250, $300, $350, and $400, for the Kindergarten $100, and for the Connecting Class, $150. The number of pupils being limited, tuition for the first half year will be charged from the opening of school in October. No deductions will be made for absence.

Afternoon classes in drawing, painting, reading, sewing, cooking and housekeeping will be begun on November 1st, and for these classes an extra charge will be made. Applications for membership in these classes should be made before October 25th. The reading classes will be conducted by Miss Chapin personally.

Miss Chapin will be at the school after September 22d, or applications may be made by letter. During the school year, Miss Chapin will be at home to parents on Tuesday afternoons.

Miss Chapin's Bulletin of Information, 1902–1903

published by the Macmillan Company. Mrs. Cartwright was generally admired, and is credited, along with Miss Chapin, with helping the girls write the school song. Miss Chapin appropriated the Eton Boating Song for the tune. As in most matters, however, she undoubtedly had a hand in the lyrics.

Miss Chapin chose the wheel as the school's symbol because it was the emblem of the erudite Saint Catherine of Alexandria, who in Christian tradition is the patron saint of philosophers, thinkers and educated women. For refusing to renounce Christianity and marry Emperor Maxentius, she was sentenced to be tortured on spiked wheels, to serve as an object lesson to other Christians. But when Catherine was fastened to the wheels, they miraculously fell apart. In *The Wheel* (the school's literary magazine) of May 1944, Class Six wrote, "The Wheel, which was broken through Catherine's faith, has become our emblem, to remind us of her courage and loyalty to her ideals." Miss Chapin, however, also saw the wheel as a symbol of education, which "has no beginning nor end, no beginning that we can remember, no end that we can see."

Chapin's motto, "Fortiter et Recte" (Bravely and Rightly), was borrowed from the Allen-Stevenson School, which had opened in 1883. Miss Chapin spoke of the motto in her 1908 speech to Chapin's first two graduates: "Fortitude, you know, includes not only courage but strength, endurance, patience, that one must learn to be brave for others as well as oneself. You know that to be true is not easy, that truth is a difficult mistress to follow."

The school prospered. By 1904, with one hundred students and twelve teachers, it had outgrown the house on Forty-seventh Street. Miss Chapin leased two houses—46 and 48 East Fifty-eighth Street—and in 1905 the school moved into these renovated quarters. Miss Chapin lived in the north rooms of number 48 with Mary Barstow Pope, the head of the Lower School. Miss Pope was a southerner and a very beautiful woman, whom the students adored. One of them wrote, "She was always smiling and very warm. I loved to watch her when she wrote on the board."

Although the quiet, residential aspect of the neighborhood was changing, and families were moving out as shops and galleries moved in, these were happy years. The school's reputation was growing. Many girls dropped out in the higher grades, but Miss Chapin's perseverance, backed by Miss Fairfax's zeal in preparing the girls for college, would eventually be rewarded. Miss Chapin wrote, "We struggled through a period of discouragement when the members of each top class, sufficiently large to be interesting and profitable, dropped off at the last moment to boarding school or other day schools because every mother became panic-stricken lest her darling should be left as the Lone Fisherman on our bit of the shore of the sea of knowledge."

Miss Chapin invited former students and older girls to come to her home on Thursday evenings. These intimate and intellectual evenings with Miss Chapin in the parlor of her brownstone evolved into an institution known as Club. Aileen Osborn Webb '10 remembered Miss Chapin reading poetry, especially Browning and Tennyson. "We would all sit enchanted by her voice and diction and her wise and amusing comments afterwards." A history of the school in *The Wheel* stated, "Club began before there was a graduating class. In fact, even before there was an Upper School, the girls who had left the school used to meet with Miss Chapin and tell her what they were doing. Then, as the school grew larger and began to have real graduating classes, the older girls and Miss Chapin used to meet at the school in the evening once a week. One of the greatest attractions of Club originally was its simplicity and friendliness, not the desire for constant, active amusement. It was a gathering where every girl could say and think what she chose, and could forget the hours of algebra problems, and the date of Nebuchadnezzar besieging Jerusalem."

Club nights were a time to read together, play games, and discuss all kinds of subjects, the "old girls" coming when they could and would. Usually, Miss Chapin read aloud, perhaps from *The Lays of Ancient Rome,* or the story *Ivan Ivanovich,* by Browning. The story of Chicken Little, another favorite, must have lightened the mood in the parlor. Charades was also popular. Lois Hall Herrick '11 remembered, "I can see Miss Chapin…being a most impressive Queen of Sheba, wearing an inverted scrap basket on her head for a crown." At the last meeting before the Christmas vacation, Miss Chapin would read Dickens's *A Christmas Carol.*

Miss Chapin also promoted athletics, not only in the school yard and gymnasium, but in a Saturday program held initially in Fort Tryon Park at the Isham family's house, and later on the playing fields of the Roger Ascham School in Hartsdale. At first, the girls traveled to the fields by coach; eventually they were provided with a private railroad car from Grand Central that was chaperoned by teachers who did their best to keep their exuberant charges under control.

The Isham House, the location of Chapin's first playground, circa 1908

Students playing basketball, circa 1910

The aprons

In the early years the school did not require uniforms, but girls and boys alike were required to wear "cream colored cotton, fitted, long sleeved, all-over aprons made at the Manhattan Trade School for Girls." (The welfare of New York City's working girls concerned Miss Chapin, and this school was of particular interest to her.) "Miss Chapin cared very much about our being simple and moral and the apron did away with competition in dress. The aprons had enormous side pockets, and so many miscellaneous things were stuffed into them that periodically they bulged way out, much to Miss Chapin's annoyance." In this case, the girls had to empty out the contents of their pockets on the room teacher's desk. One might find, along with pencils and erasers and linen handkerchiefs, "compacts of Dorin face powder, marcel-wave hair curlers, 'rats' to put under our pompadours, bone staves to hold up high collars of our shirtwaists, [and] class rings and pins, not only of our own school, but of Groton and St. Paul's."

In 1905 Miss Chapin set up a new science laboratory in one of the basement kitchens. She had ardently wished for adequate teaching of science in her school, and this makeshift laboratory was the first step. The houses did have their drawbacks. The fuel bunkers were so small that coal was poured incessantly. The street was narrow, and high apartments on the opposite side blocked the light. In addition, the noise of motor engines all but drowned out the children's recitations. School

The school, 1908

started at 9:00 A.M. and ended at 1:15 P.M. Most girls were either driven to school in their family's car by the chauffeur, or walked with their fathers on their way to the office. The girls brought their recess snack with them. Modest treats such as plain peanut butter sandwiches and unfrosted cake were allowed, but the First Class teacher kept a knife to scrape off any forbidden jam or chocolate frosting. By the last period, the girls were ravenous. As one alumna recalled, "We used to have reading the last class before we went home, and we'd sit in the dining room…and all these wonderful smells from the kitchen, where Miss Chapin's and Miss Pope's lunch was being prepared, would waft up toward us."

In the early years of the school, the world of comfortable brownstones seemed established and safe. Children could romp in the parks and walk to school unchaperoned, although most Chapin girls were chaperoned. Maud Cabot Morgan '21 wrote, "I recollect the walk to school…. There was a sense that everybody was going where they had to go, be it school or business, and that there was plenty of time to get there. Beyond being on time for meals, haste was not a word I associate with my childhood." Young Chapin girls played prisoner's base on the south end of the Central Park Mall or went to Huyler's on Forty-third Street "for ice cream sodas and glass punch cups filled with chocolate ice cream topped by marsh-mallow sauce." They skated at Iceland and took piano lessons and dancing lessons. Catherine Watjen Pemberton '20 remembered a New York that was "perfectly charming. There were very few tall buildings and there were trees on most of the blocks." But tall buildings were being built. The area around the school became less residential at the start of the new century. The University Club was built in 1899, the St. Regis Hotel in 1905, and the Rizzoli Building, the first commercial building in the area, in 1907. The great mansions began to shut down. The Vanderbilt mansions, which had been built between 1879 and 1882, transforming Fifth Avenue from Fifty-first to Fifty-eighth Street, were constructed to last for generations but didn't survive even one. In only fifteen years these palaces became bunkers, besieged by hotel developers and swarms of people and vehicles. Progress, in the form of skyscrapers, commerce, the automobile and a booming economy, began to alter the safe, comfortable brownstone era in which the girls had grown up.

Such rapid change reflected the energy and belief in the future that characterized the beginning of the twentieth century. As the economy boomed, along Madison and Fifth Avenues and on parts of Park Avenue twenty-year-old brownstones were torn down to make way for Beaux-Arts and Renaissance-style town houses.

In 1909, to accommodate her expanding student population, Miss Chapin decided to buy two brownstones, at 32 and 34 East Fifty-seventh Street, and the school moved in 1910. Despite some personal misgivings, Edward Henderson helped her make the down payment. He need not have worried about his investment. Miss Chapin sold the buildings in 1928 for more than twice their original cost. In real estate as well as edu-cation, Miss Chapin displayed remarkable acumen.

Alumnae remember the new school, which combined the two town houses, with real affection. Elsie Barber Trask '25 said, "I remember the two brownstones near the corner of Fifty-seventh Street. There was a big square stoop where mothers used to wait to pick us up." The buildings were connected by a grand staircase that led up from the main hall to the second-floor corridors, which led to the homerooms and narrow

32-34 East Fifty-seventh Street

The south side of Fifty-seventh Street in 1910, looking west from Park Avenue toward Madison Avenue. The school is at the far end of the row of brownstones.

classrooms that had been hall bedrooms. There were two staircases from the second floor on up with connecting doors at the top and bottom of each stairway. Alumnae recall the building's "highly polished brown woodwork, the brown sepia prints on the tan walls, the brown chairs and desks." The desks were old-fashioned, with lids and inkwells.

The entrance hall was dominated by the wide staircase, with invitingly wide banisters. Initially, the Assembly Room, Eleanor King Ames '18 recalled, "was in two parts (probably originally the parlor and dining room of one old brownstone house). The students stood in the front room while Miss Chapin led the morning prayers from the rear room, which I believe also served as her office." In a short time these two rooms were combined into one Assembly Room with a small stage or platform at the south end. The ceiling was low, and because the windows were kept shut to keep out the noise, the room was often stuffy. Fainting during Prayers was a common occurrence. "The whole school could just fit in when standing in close ranks."

The school eventually expanded into two rented floors in 36 East Fifty-seventh Street, where there was a restaurant, the Russian Eagle, in the basement with a doorman wearing the uniform of a Cossack. An alumna reported, "Occasionally the Cossack, sent up with a message, opened the wrong door and enormously enlivened the class into which he burst."

The basement was dark and plain, but it was equipped with a science laboratory. The backyard was covered with concrete and had basketball nets on each side of it. There was a fire escape in back, and Miss Chapin staged numerous fire drills because, it was rumored, she wanted to show off her girls. Catherine Watjen Pemberton recalls her reaction to a drill and the instructions of Ethel Grey Stringfellow, who at the time was a beloved young teacher. "I'll never forget the fire drill because I had a fear of heights that was beyond anything. I think I'd burn to death before I went down that fire escape. But we were all supposed to go down that fire escape outside the window. Miss Stringfellow saw me cowering in the background…and she said, 'Catherine, you lead,' and I did."

All twelve classes led a close and disciplined existence. The school day began with Prayers. Afterward the girls would go to their various

Banner presentation in the Fifty-seventh Street yard, Miss Chapin at center, circa 1911

Early days on Fifty-seventh Street

classrooms and the academic part of the day proceeded, interrupted with a midmorning break. Classroom hours were from 9:00 to 12:30 for the Lower School, and to 1:00 and 1:15 for the Middle and Upper Schools respectively. Pupils were permitted to return between 2:30 and 4:30 to study under the supervision of a teacher or for athletics. Sometimes this was obligatory. Eleanor King Ames remembered that "lunches were never served at school, so those of us who wished to stay for daily athletics in the afternoons brought our own. A sandwich (yes, usually peanut butter) and an apple was the standard menu, with milk supplied by the school." Girls who stayed to practice for the choir on Friday afternoons undoubtedly did the same. School opened the first week of October and closed the end of May. There was a week off at Christmas, another at Easter, and a long Thanksgiving weekend. As for tuition, the cost of Kindergarten started at $150 for the year, with $50 increments added to succeeding classes until the sum reached $500.

The curriculum, which had been expanding as new grades and new students were added, now became formalized. By 1911, art, English, history, mathematics, science, Latin, French, German and diction were offered in both the Middle and Upper Schools along with optional afternoon classes in drawing, painting, sewing and cooking. Before long college entrance examinations were being taken in history, English and mathematics, and in 1913 four girls passed the entrance examinations for Bryn Mawr College. One of these, Margaret Henderson Bailie, graduated from Bryn Mawr in 1917 and is recognized as Chapin's first college graduate. In the Upper School, the girls were divided around 1914 into either the General or the College Division. General Division girls were not obliged to take as much mathematics, Latin or Greek as those in the College Division, but they did study chemistry, art, history and English. Their college-bound classmates concentrated on geometry, algebra, French, Latin, American history, English and physics. There was no stigma attached to being a General Division student. So few girls went on to college that it was considered rather peculiar to do so. In fact, the education a girl received as a General Division student was excellent and in many ways preferable to that of the College Division. The French course for the General girls seems to have been more practical, as it concentrated more on ideas and the ability to speak the language than on grammar.

Miss Chapin, in addition to her administrative duties, knew and taught every child in the school. She supervised News in the Lower School, taught her outline of history in the Fourth Class, taught reading to Classes Five, Six and Seven, Shakespeare to Class Eight, history to Classes Nine through Eleven and Dante to Class Twelve.

Parents respected and liked Miss Chapin. She excelled at public relations, could get along with anybody and had many connections. Her

Miss Chapin on reading

Miss Chapin, circa 1911

Miss Chapin, 1922

passion for literature, opera and drama and her ability to inspire made her, at the least, a satisfying companion and, at best, an exhilarating one. She rated very high marks as a teacher. Miss Stringfellow later characterized her as "the most brilliant teacher…and the most cultivated person I think I have ever known." A student wrote, "I can see her now as she stood before us in those wonderful history classes—a truly commanding presence. Without making the slightest concession to feminine vanity, she was undoubtedly very handsome. Her hair was white, drawn straight back from the forehead into the tightest of knots. A short straight nose and firm mouth and chin gave austerity to a face lighted by large, wide apart, clear eyes and softened by a youthful pink and white complexion. Her figure was of medium height and stocky, but the erectness of her carriage and set of her head and shoulders lent height and stature beyond physical measure. As a principal, she could be stern and frightening, particularly to a transgressor; as a teacher, she could be inspirational; as a friend and counsellor, she made her mark for life."

As Eleanor King Ames wrote, "Miss Chapin was strict, but fair. In our younger days, though we admired and respected her greatly, we were rather in awe of her. As we grew older, however, we got to know her better and by the time we had her as our history teacher in the Twelfth Class, we had become very fond of her. I look back with deep gratitude to her great dedication in trying to draw out the best in each one of her pupils. She had the highest ideals, educationally and personally, and tried to give us strong guidelines of right and wrong to go by, and showed real interest in each individual's future plans."

The good of the child always came first. She told her teachers: "Learn from the children. Watch and study the children in our care, and fit the child for his work and the work to the child. Take out the child—the problem of the individual child—and most of us would rather run a loom in a factory than teach. Never sacrifice a child to a class, nor a class to a method, nor a result to the honor and glory of the school."

During the 1910–1911 school year there occurred two accidents, one tragic and one with lingering effects, which should be mentioned. Miss Chapin and her friend and colleague, Miss Pope, were traveling uptown by trolley. As their trolley passed Grand Central, where men were excavating a tunnel, there was a dreadful explosion. Miss Pope's niece, Audrey Hedge '27, said many years later, "The pipes blew up. Miss Chapin got a wound in her head, and a pipe killed my aunt. It was terrible." Miss Chapin was out of school for six months, emotionally devastated.

Miss Pope's death marked the end of Miss Chapin's youthful gaiety; students remember her as becoming quieter. Not long after the accident, when Miss Chapin had returned to her full duties at the school, she met with another disaster. She was sitting in her office behind the Assembly Room when the plaster ceiling gave way and a great chunk of it came down on her. An alumna who was sitting in her sewing class that day remembered, "There was a terrific crash. We rushed in from the little pantry and there was the ceiling on the floor and Miss Chapin just going out the door. I believe her shoulder was hit, and that she always had headaches after that." Miss Chapin may have had headaches, but she continued to display the courage that she inspired in others.

Over and over again she stressed the importance of moral courage. "Apprehensiveness can chill any ardor, can make anyone of us an idler, and a laggard. If we are brave, we know that either failure or success may serve our need…. Courage that rises anew from despair and that undertakes, despite all tribulations, to overcome the world, such courage is one of the central treasures of moral life." She urged her graduates to have definite ambitions, not to dissipate their talents. "If you are conscious that in one field you can do better work and with greater happiness than in any other, make it your own at once! Try when you rise, always to lift some one with you, or to make life richer and more beautiful for others because of your triumph."

CHAPTER TWO

TRADITIONS

We were taught ethics.
ELIZABETH GAY PIERCE '25

Miss Chapin had a talent for bringing in remarkable women to teach at the school, who themselves came to shape the traditions of the school. She selected them for their training, experience and background. In her 1925 letter to the alumnae of Miss Abbott's School she wrote, "No woman should attempt to teach professionally until she has prepared for her work by study and pedagogical training. Yes, interpreted, this does mean that I would not employ my young self in my own school today."

Among these teachers, none was more formidable than Mary Cecelia Fairfax. In the same letter to Miss Abbott's School alumnae, Miss Chapin wrote, "A year after the beginning of Miss Chapin's School, Miss Mary Cecelia Fairfax, the most important teacher of the earlier school, joined its faculty. A few years later Miss Fairfax became my partner and Associate Head of the School. A trained teacher of unusual ability and a very exceptional person in many ways, her contribution to the school cannot be overestimated."

Miss Fairfax was born in Prince George's County, Maryland, on December 26, 1871, the daughter of John Contee Fairfax, eleventh

The Class of 1918 with Miss Chapin at Field Day

Mary Cecelia Fairfax

baron of Cameron in the Scottish peerage, and Mary Kirby Fairfax. She was educated in private schools, and was then graduated from the Potsdam Normal Training School in upstate New York. (A normal school was a school for training and certifying teachers.) In 1906 Miss Chapin put her in charge of supervising the Upper School and designing the college preparatory curriculum; in 1911, shortly after the death of Miss Pope, she made Miss Fairfax her partner, and in 1913, associate headmistress.

Miss Fairfax was undoubtedly Miss Chapin's right hand, a perfect foil to her New England employer. Miss Stringfellow commented that "Miss Fairfax was very practical and Miss Chapin was an idealist." Both ladies were aristocratic, but Miss Chapin was sociable, whereas Miss Fairfax was shy. Miss Fairfax had curly blond hair and was very pretty. Elizabeth Mason Walbridge '35 described her as "very quiet, but she was the keystone in developing academic excellence. She was strict about our college entrance exams and college performance. She gave us mathematics the hard way." She was also an avid gardener and gave the school a greenhouse. A slate plaque, designed by Margaret Henderson Bailie, still sets a cool, contemplative tone there with its inscription, "a green thought in a green shade," a quotation from Andrew Marvell's poem "The Garden." Miss Fairfax gardened enthusiastically after she and Miss Chapin moved to their house in Turtle Bay. Margaret Henderson Bailie spoke of her as being "frenzied" about it; she sat at the table "champing to get out and get to work while Miss Chapin cheerfully but firmly insisted on finishing her luncheon." Katharine Walker MacKenty '23 recalled a farmer driving into the city with loads of manure from the Walker pony stables in Scarsdale. In receipt of the gift, Miss Fairfax's eyes twinkled as she exclaimed, "Such nice, fresh manure!"

Miss Fairfax could be fierce with the girls, perhaps because of a slight speech impediment, which caused her *R*'s to come out as *W*'s. An alumna recalled, "She didn't dare be nice for fear girls would take advantage of her. She went so far the other way her students were terrified of her." Still, another alumna remembered her as "a wonderful little person . . . very definite and brilliant."

Ethel Grey Stringfellow, who was to become Miss Fairfax's successor and the school's third headmistress, began her career at Chapin in 1909. Miss Stringfellow was born on May 31, 1887, in Tuscaloosa, Alabama, to Lucy Haskins and James Horace Stringfellow, both from

Members of the Class of 1939 in the greenhouse planting their summer gardens

Virginia. James Stringfellow was an Episcopal minister, and Ethel, along with her two sisters and two brothers, was brought up strictly. Miss Stringfellow attended Noble Institute in Anniston, Alabama, and received her diploma from the State Normal School in Florence, Alabama, in 1906. Before coming to New York, she taught during the 1906–1907 school year in the public schools in Birmingham.

In 1909 Miss Stringfellow received her B.S. degree from Teachers College at Columbia University and began teaching at Miss Chapin's School. She first taught in the Lower School, then went on to teach in the Middle School, eventually becoming its head. From her earliest days in the school, Ethel Stringfellow's hearty laugh and good humor endeared her to the students; yet, she never had a problem with discipline. Over and over, her former students recall that she seldom lost her temper, and that, instead, she used humor to defuse a problem and drive home the point she wanted to make. Years later this ability would serve her well as headmistress. Jane Watson Crane '23 summed up Miss Stringfellow nicely: "She was the most wonderful thing that could happen to a fifth-grader."

Miss Stringfellow

A member of the Class of 1937 recalled, "We worked hard over our [arithmetic] problems because if we had a perfect lesson we would be rewarded by a magnificent scroll of red crayon from Miss Stringfellow's own hand."

Having Miss Stringfellow as a teacher was almost like having somebody your own age who understood you. She had such an excellent sense of fun. A student remembers her very black hair and slim figure. Throughout her career as an educator she delighted—when the occa-

Miss Wilkinson, in perhaps her most famous pose, 1950

sion merited—in dancing a cakewalk. A student recalled, "My most wonderful memory of her is at Club, at Teachers' Night. She did a cakewalk, and she had long arms and legs, you know, and she was wonderful! She'd throw her head back and sing."

Miss Stringfellow's "Budget" course for the Elevens was as popular as it was useful. In this course the girls learned how to do double-entry bookkeeping, to keep a budget, plan menus, order food and furnish a home. Miss Stringfellow told her students that they should earn at least $18.50 a week in order to be self-sufficient. For the college-bound, she gave a brief course in economics, in which she lectured the girls on stocks and bonds and advised them to get a mortgage when buying a house. Yet it wasn't Miss Stringfellow's sound advice that endeared her to the girls; it was her genuine affection for them and her belief that they should have fun while they were being educated.

Another important figure in the early years of the school was Katharine May Wilkinson. She was, she claimed, the same height as Napoleon, and she possessed a great deal of his flair and boldness. Educated by tutors at home, then a graduate of Smith College, she came to Chapin in 1904 and remained until 1952, reappearing as an assistant librarian in 1953–1954.

Miss Wilkinson's history classes were legendary. She used Miss Chapin's famous history outlines and time charts, and reenacted each battle and climactic event, thereby making what might have been dull, gray facts spring vibrantly to life. She was incapable of being boring. A student wrote, "I used to have study hour when she taught the Eleventh Class, and I wouldn't do any studying. I just listened to the class. It was fascinating. I learned quite a lot of history that way." She loved to tell stories, and her students adored hearing them. One favorite was about the king of Persia, Cambyses II, who, when he was attempting to conquer Egypt in 525 B.C., gave his troops kittens to throw at the Egyptians. Cats were sacred to the Egyptians, and they rushed to put the kittens away to safety. By the time that was done, they were overrun.

In the February 1949 *Wheel,* Betty Wei Liu '49, later to become a Chapin history teacher herself, penned this delightful tribute to Miss Wilkinson:

What does outstanding mean? Of course it is as good as the other English words, but can you use some other ones like distinguished, marvelous or excellent instead of outstanding?

She is wonderful; she is marvelous, and she is an excellent teacher. I shall always remember the presidents of the United States because she taught me that if you "Polk a Taylor he'll Fillmore Pierce Buchanan cars. Then Lincoln and the rest are easy." I shall remember, too, that the constitution starts with a preamble, and the preamble begins "We, the people," but not, "We, the states." Nor will any of us be able to forget the Rhyme of the English Kings!

THE RHYME OF THE ENGLISH KINGS
First William the Norman, then William, his son,
Henry, Stephen and Henry, then Richard and John,
Then Henry III, Edwards I, II and III
And again after Richard, three Henrys we see.
Two Edwards, third Richard, if rightly I guess,
Two Henrys, sixth Edward, Queen Mary, Queen Bess.
Then Jamie, the Scotsman, and Charles whom they slew
But received after Cromwell another Charles II.
Then James II ascended the throne
Till William and Mary together came on.
Then Anne, Georges four and William all passed.
God gave us Queen Vic, may her fame ever last.

And after Victoria's long reign was done
We see Edward VII and George V, his son.
Then Edward the VIII who gave up his crown
To his brother George VI, may he reign with renown.

Nor would Miss Wilkinson's students ever forget her formula for a good term paper. "Like a lady's skirt, it should be long enough to cover the subject and short enough to be interesting."

Margaret Emerson Bailey came to Chapin in 1909 from Rhode Island via Bryn Mawr and her desk at the *New York Times* as a night reporter. An accomplished minor poet and novelist, she was a descendant of Ralph Waldo Emerson, a member of the Poetry Society and a friend of Robert Frost.

To her students, it seemed that Miss Bailey personally knew every novelist alive. She had great distinction of mind and taste. She selected only the best in literature, whether classical or modern, and inspired her students to appreciate and strive for excellence. (In her honor the Class of 1925 raised special funds for awards in creative writing to be known as the Margaret Emerson Bailey Prizes, which are still given annually.) As one student recalled, "She smoked, her hair was puffy and she wore a hat perched on it with a feather going up. She was always trailing a scarf or something behind…but she always conducted a perfect class." One of Miss Bailey's last students painted a poignant picture of the aging teacher. "She had once been a beauty, but then had become somewhat blousy and

Miss Bailey, 1918

faded. The white lace jabot at her throat was soiled, her clothes rumpled, her fingers deeply stained with nicotine. Rumored to have danced with Douglas MacArthur at West Point, and to have gone out on the town with New York's notorious mayor, Jimmy Walker, she had written a novel, a thinly veiled autobiography in which she had rejected a romantic suitor, I believe a first cousin, because the bloodlines were too

Miss Morison

One of Miss Stewart's bird walks,
The Wheel, May 1939

similar. Obviously, as a woman with a past, she was an object of much speculation and considerable admiration."

While Miss Bailey supplied the dash and drama in English that the girls adored, Margaret Morison, who came to Chapin in 1919, taught them grammar. She was serious in class and treated her students as "partners in the search for expression." She sympathized with her students' struggles with the written word and gently encouraged them to persevere. Miss Morison was a lovely-looking woman with a compassionate nature whose impeccable standards impressed her students.

E. Grace Stewart, who came to Chapin in 1911, will go down in history as the teacher who led generations of Chapin girls on bird walks. She was indefatigable, theatrical and full of exhilaration. As one student wrote, "Miss Stewart opened my eyes to the wonder of nature, especially in one's own back yard, to the need to protect our environment and to the interdependence of all forms of life. Miss Stewart's classes were not as scientific as those offered today, but she instilled in her pupils a love and reverence for nature which has influenced my life."

Prior to her Chapin career, Miss Stewart had studied biology at Teachers College, Columbia University. Before attending Teachers College, she had taught for eleven years at a public school in Johnstown, Pennsylvania. In 1891, during the Johnstown flood, she had floated down the river on the roof of her house.

Cramped for space and low on equipment, Miss Stewart settled in to teach the girls the basics of natural science. "In 1912 I was told I should teach a class in physics. The equipment on hand was one vacuum pump, a Leyden jar, an electrophorus and piece of fur, three magnets, a compass, two telegraphy keys, some battery jars and zinc plates, and a barometer that was out of order. I bought a book on home-made apparatus and went to work." A student wrote, "She was a very pleasant person to study under, the same to everyone. She kept the laboratory very neatly and always explained everything so well."

Miss Stewart's students remember her science classes as shaped by her own passions. As far as sex education went, Miss Stewart taught the girls about bees and the pollination of flowers and left it at that. Birds were her real love. In one of her letters to the school after her retirement she wrote, "If you are interested in birds, you become interested in the conservation of our world." Her famous bird walks began at what is now the Loeb Boathouse in Central Park, and then continued up through the Ramble. Naturally her charges did not always behave or show much interest in birds, but nonetheless generations of them became bird watchers. Many years later Barbara Childs Lawrence '30 organized an annual birding expedition in Central Park in memory of Miss Stewart, with breakfast at the Loeb Boathouse restaurant afterward.

Miss Stewart was the driving force behind the creation of Chapin's Audubon Club in April of 1922. Anne Morrow Lindbergh '24 was one of the first students to pay her twenty-five-cent dues and become a member. At one of the first meetings of the club, Mr. Avis gave an illustrated lecture on birds and imitated many bird songs; a year later the girls held a bird party to which everyone came dressed as a bird.

Grace Yates arrived at the school in 1911. "Oh, boy, she was a humdinger!" one alumna exclaimed of Miss Yates. Trained at Wellesley, and a pioneer in physical education for girls, she promptly replaced the classes of graceful calisthenics with rigorous gymnastics and outdoor games. "Miss Yates put us through inhuman tortures on the horizontal bars in the gym," one student recalled. She reigned over the gym and

Miss Yates at the Hartsdale station

Miss Yates with students at Hartsdale

games in the yard, "worried over our posture and strengthened our muscles with rhythmic exercises, which we did lying prone on mats." She also taught yoga. "We'd begin with breathing exercises and then we'd stand on our heads, and hang on the rings and bars." Student posture was also of great concern to Miss Chapin. An alumna recalled, "She appointed Miss Yates to go the rounds daily to each classroom, pad and pencil in hand, and give a black mark to every girl found slumping at her work." Miss Yates was instrumental in designing the school uniform, and in setting up the Saturday games at Hartsdale. She also organized the Greek Games, where the entire school dressed in flowing robes to perform dramatic and athletic feats.

Anne Kendall came to the school in 1906 and developed the Lower School. She enjoyed dramatics and revealed considerable artistic talent in the Lower School projects she initiated. There were pageants galore. One alumna recalled, "There were wonderful plays in the backyard. I remember being part of a dragon. We came down the fire escape into the yard. Another time we had a play on Norse mythology." Diana McIlvaine '34 remembers a Chinese play in the yard where Miss Yates shot off a rocket. "She did all the sprays and comets and everything. It was a miracle!"

The Lower School students loved Miss Kendall. When a student misbehaved she would put her arms around her as she scolded her. More than once her students organized exclusive clubs for nefarious purposes. Miss Kendall suggested they merge all the classes' clubs into one supreme organization that would be motivated by the highest ideals. As one former student recalled, "These were, summarily, to keep the room in immaculate order. The idea was accepted grudgingly, but eventually we even became quite excited over the various committees. There was a Committee to Push the Chairs, a Committee to Tidy the Shelves, a Committee to Pick up the Floor, and innumerable others."

Julia Wilde, the assistant treasurer, arrived at the school in 1903 and retired in 1941. Miss Stringfellow wrote of this remarkable lady, "Miss Wilde from 1903 on did all the correspondence, received and disbursed the funds, gathered the data on pupils and parents for Miss Chapin, registered the children when accepted, and, in the early years, even looked down their throats if they were suspected of measles or other contagious diseases. When the school was incorporated, Miss Wilde kept all the records, and again, when it was moved to the new building in 1928, she saw that the packing and transfer of books and all classroom materials were in order.... A vast amount of personal and academic work for Miss Chapin, too, Miss Wilde carried on as a matter of course. No matter what personal sacrifice it entailed, nothing was too much trouble if it was for the best interest of the school."

Miss Chapin and the remarkable cast of characters that she assembled came to shape a unique institution. Chapin alumnae recall with nostalgia the school's traditions, which have added color and substance to the academic day through the years. Prayers, Bible verses, News, dates, the adding board, Thanksgiving and Christmas rituals, Club, the ongoing rivalry with Brearley and especially the uniform—all are affectionately remembered.

One of the earliest of the traditions was Prayers, which Miss Chapin had begun while she was still a teacher at Primary Classes for Girls. It was here that she set the moral and religious tone of the school. The girls would march into the Assembly Room to a rousing tune, such as the triumphal march from *Aida*. As Eleanor King Ames remembered, "The hymn for each day was printed on a large banner above our heads, and the choir stood on the platform facing the rest of the school, as did Miss Chapin. We said the Lord's Prayer, and each week we had to learn verses from the Bible. Much to our terror, whenever they sounded thin when recited in unison, Miss Chapin would call upon individuals [to recite]. The shorter girls took refuge behind those who were taller. As I was just under six feet there was no escape for me, so it became a necessity for me always to know the verses!"

In later years the alumnae treasured their Bible verses. According to one, "Bible verses helped place roots in my life." Another remarked, "Though I didn't get much meaning out of them then, they've been wonderful to hold on to." Perhaps the most dramatic testimonial to their value came from Miss Stringfellow, who told the story of Ellen Biddle Stackelberg '30, who had married a German before World War II. "The [foreign-born] wives of German soldiers were put into a house near Munich next to a French prison camp. Ellen was one of them. When the Gestapo discovered the women were helping the French soldiers to escape, they took the women and held them for days. Ellen wrote, 'The thing that carried me through that awful experience was the Bible verses I learned at the Chapin School. I said them over and over again, and taught them to the wives of the other men.' "

BIBLE VERSES
RECITED DURING
THE SEVENTY-FIFTH
ANNIVERSARY YEAR

King James Version

St. Matthew 5: 1–6
St. Matthew 5: 7–16
Genesis 1: 1–5
Isaiah 2: 4
Ecclesiastes 3: 1–8
Psalm 147
St. Luke 2: 1–20
St. Matthew 2: 1–6
Proverbs 3: 13–14
Psalm 100
St. Matthew 7: 7–8
St. John 15: 12–14
I Corinthians 13: 1–13
Psalm 23
St. John 14: 1–6, 27
St. Matthew 6: 24–29
Numbers 6: 24–26
St. Matthew 11: 28–30
Psalm 121

THE CHAPIN SCHOOL DATES
(revised in 1975)

B.C.

c. 3000	Pyramid Age began First Calendar in Egypt
c. 1720	Hammurabi's Code of Laws in Babylon
c. 1600	Golden Age of Cretan Civilization
1000	David, King of the Hebrews
c. 800	Homer and the *Iliad*
c. 776	The First Olympiad
753	Rome founded

For complete dates, see pages 156–157.

GOD OUR FATHER

God our Father made the daylight,
God our Father made the night.
God made mountains, sea, and sky
And the white clouds floating high.

God we thank Thee for the showers,
God we thank thee for the dew.
Mighty trees and flowers small,
God our Father gave them all.

Another legacy from Primary Classes, and from Miss Abbott's School before that, was News, a Friday "General Exercise" period, in which the girls gained practice in public speaking. News is remembered both as a triumph and an agony. Priscilla Stanton Auchincloss recalled, "On Fridays after Prayers we used to have to speak to the whole school. Perhaps warned a week ahead, it was very good for the shy."

The memorization of dates without the historical background to pin them on would seem intolerably dry today, but the dates came to be cherished by the alumnae. The dates were also vitally important to Miss Chapin. She wrote, "And dates! Five dates a week for every week of the school year, reviewed each year during the five years of the Upper School until my girls, in spite of all temptation to forget about every nation, can't help automatically saying 'Death of Socrates' when somebody punches the button 399 B.C. Rumour says that a brilliant young graduate of ours won her erudite young Polish husband by murmuring unconsciously '1648' when he alluded to the Treaty of Westphalia."

Unlike the dates, the adding board—and Miss Fairfax before it with a pointer—was the stuff of nightmares. One description, entitled "A Useful Tool," tells of a board about three feet high and two feet wide. On it were six horizontal columns of numbers, which could be changed to show different combinations of figures. Pupils were asked to add them. At the end of their Twelfth Class year, they had to do this in front of the whole Upper School, while being timed, to see who was the fastest. As one alumna recalled, "The number board was a terror. We had to add it up in under a minute in front of the school in order to graduate." However, Anne Finch Cox '36 said that the adding board taught her not to be afraid of long columns of numbers and to enjoy arithmetic. "It was a boon. I can always add up my grocery list before paying quicker than an adding machine."

Other customs started in the first years of the school were the annual Thanksgiving and Christmas programs. At early Thanksgiving programs, the girls brought gifts of food, which were distributed to a church in Harlem. No Chapin girls will forget the cheerful melody of "We Gather Together" or "God Our Father" sung each year at Thanksgiving as the Lower School files up to the stage with its precariously balanced offering of oranges and apples. The November 1984 issue of *Limelight,* the student newspaper, describes the tradition in its more recent glory: "On the day before Thanksgiving we attend an all-school Prayers, where we sing traditional hymns. On the stage assemble the

Thanksgiving Prayers, 1977

To Thee, O Lord, our thanks are due
For Thy great gift of life,
For harvests now instead of want
And peace instead of strife,
For love and mercy shown by Thee
In sending down Thy Son
To tell us how to live and serve
Until our work be done.

Save us, dear Lord, from hate and sin
To which we often yield,
Teach us to love as Thou did'st love
The children Thou dost shield.
Not only for ourselves do we
Make prayers to Thee today
But also for the friends we help
To keep Thanksgiving Day.

And now to Thee the children bring
The harvest's golden store,
That Thou may'st bless its fruitfulness
For those whose need is sore.
We give Thee thanks, O God, that we
May give these gifts of love,
And make this day a festival,
Of praise to Thee above.

Lower Schoolers, complete with green-and-white striped uniforms and handmade Indian headdresses. After they march out to the applause of their enthusiastic schoolmates, the magnificent display of hundreds of containers of food is visible. Every Chapinite brings in a few cans of food for the poor to eat on Thanksgiving. Two days before the holiday a large group of Middle and Upper Schoolers gather to arrange this food in rows and columns on the stage."

The Christmas traditions were even more elaborate, according to Katharine Walker MacKenty:

Christmas holiday time at the school began in December with Advent and the daily unfolding of St. Luke's story of The Nativity through the Bible verses recited in Prayers. Shortly before vacation, the Christmas play was given for the school and parents in the Assembly Room. The productions were planned carefully and many parents loaned beautiful embroidered robes to dignify the Wise Men. The stage was small, but the angels found room to sing, as did the entire audience, after the solemn procession to the manger. At our last assembly before we left for the holidays, we gave Miss Chapin her Christmas present. Each girl brought a silver or gold dollar for the sack that was presented to Miss Chapin by a member of the youngest class. This gift went to the Manhattan Trade School for Girls.

ONE NIGHT WHEN STARS WERE SHINING

One night when stars were shining,
And shepherds watched their sheep
A mother laid her baby
Where the oxen sleep.
Mary was that mother,
Christ her baby fair,
Angels sang for gladness
Because the Lord was there.

Carol, carol children, carol joyfully,
Carol, carol children, carol merrily.

God sent down that Christ Child
From home in Heaven above,
To teach all little children
How to live and love.
So this happy Christmas
Sing your carols bright,
Sing to all the story
Of that first Christmas night.

Carol, carol children, carol joyfully,
Carol, carol children, carol merrily.

Members of the Class of 1997 singing "The Friendly Beasts," 1985

Eleanor King Ames later wrote, "After several Christmases, when Miss Chapin had received countless penwipers, handkerchiefs and calendars, she said that if anyone wished to give her a Christmas present, she would rather have a dollar which she would like to give to the Manhattan Trade School towards a scholarship fund. I remember the year when it was my turn to collect this, I walked down Park Avenue to school with $300 in *gold* in a small suitcase, and kept looking behind me all the way to see if I was being followed!"

Katherine Post Mason '19 remembered all 250 girls coming together for the Christmas Assembly. "Miss Stringfellow would lead the Lower School down the stairs singing 'One Night When Stars Were Shining' and we would join in as they arrived." Through much of Chapin's history, the Lower School plays wove endless variations on the theme of the shepherds, the angel Gabriel and the Mother and Child. Beginning about 1970 the theme was broadened and became more secular.

Club nights, a unique tradition, followed their own Christmas patterns. During Thursday evenings in December the girls gathered in the library to sew and fill candy bags for St. Cyprion's Mission or some other worthy charity, while Miss Chapin read aloud *A Christmas Carol*. The bags were made of pieces of heavy cheesecloth, sewn together on three sides and filled with candy. A ribbon was then woven through the fourth side. Toys, given to the mission by the Middle School, would be wrapped and packed. On a separate night, the girls would gather to sing traditional Christmas carols, including Miss Chapin's favorite, the French carol "Minuit Chrétien."

The uniform was of overwhelming importance to the Chapin student. Uniforms evolved a few years after the arrival of Miss Yates, who insisted the girls could not do their exercises properly because the skirts of the day were so narrow that the girls could not move their legs around. Miss Wilkinson wrote, "A heavy, hot, green uniform was adopted in 1914 over the protests of mothers who said that with a uniform their daughters never wore their pretty frocks." Miss Stringfellow described the uniform as a pleated skirt that was vast enough to accom-

modate the enormous bloomers, when they were worn underneath. A blouse, tie and belted jacket completed the ensemble. Lower and Middle School girls wore one-piece V-necked tunics over bloomers and a blouse with a tie. All this was intricately and securely fastened to specially buttoned underwear. As one alumna reported, "The Lower School 'Posture League' underwaists were designed by Dr. Joel Goldthwaite of Boston to remove the weight of the clothing from the shoulders and so improve the posture of small children. [They] buttoned down the front, then special underpants buttoned onto that. Then our bloomers buttoned again onto this, and over that went the jumper."

With the uniform the girls wore black lisle stockings and specially ordered flat, black laced shoes. Miss Chapin was distressed by the Upper School girls' predilection for French heels, and the school instructions sent

Students in the Fifty-seventh Street yard, circa 1915

In uniform: Augusta Trimble '22 and Rosamond Borland '21

to parents during the summer warned that there were many cases of "weak feet, which we are trying to correct through exercises, and each pupil will be required to wear while in school a low-heeled oxford shoe with sensible toe." The Upper School girls were allowed a broad, one-inch heel. Shoes had to be low-cut to allow free circulation and the use of the foot and ankle muscles. No jewelry or makeup, except for powder, was allowed. A Club-night skit featured the following song about the uniform:

When I first put this uniform on, I said as I looked at the class,
There cannot be many, I doubt if there are any this figure and form
  can surpass.
Indeed we are free of mistakes if these uniforms tout women's shapes.
Though all this is witty, not even the pretty show classic intelligent taste.

Another Chapin tradition, the Alumnae Association, was born in the fall of 1914, when a group of alumnae met at the school. The Alumnae Association held annual meetings from that time on; they were often addressed by outside speakers who were leaders in community service. By 1917 the alumnae had formed committees, each one "to acquaint itself with various opportunities in New York City...any alumna desiring information about business courses, dramatic work, music schools, literature or art classes should go to that committee and there find out just where she could best effect what she wished to do."

World War I sharpened the girls' awareness of the plight of the less fortunate. Money in the Alumnae Association treasury was given to the cause "voted the best presented and the most worthy. Thus it came about that in 1917 we gave $100 to the Baroness de Rancoigne for milk for children in Belgium."

The origin of the Chapin colors, green and gold, is not documented. From early on, however, sports teams were divided into Greens and Golds, and the rivalry between them was fierce. At the end of the year, one team would proudly win the school banner. Sisters were always assigned the same color, and when alumnae daughters began coming to Chapin, they were assigned to the same team as their mothers. Katharine Walker MacKenty explained: "We were never allowed to compete with other schools in athletics, but there was great rivalry between our own Green and Gold teams."

Miss Yates founded the Athletic Association in 1911. Its mission statement read, "The Athletic Association includes the groups of girls who join this Association with the intention of going as regularly as possible to the School Playgrounds on Saturdays." Eleanor King Ames recalled, "For those of us who liked athletics, we greatly looked forward to spending all day each Saturday at 'The Playground' at Hartsdale. It took about an hour each way by train. There was a comfortable rambling old country house, a bountiful hot lunch and enough land to use for field hockey, basketball, softball, archery, etc.—even for skiing,

Field Day, circa 1915

Miss Chapin at Field Day, circa 1912

Eleanor King Ames '18 running the hurdles, Field Day, May 12, 1917

Field Day, circa 1912

which we did without poles and with wildly waving arms. A Field Day [beginning in 1912] was held there each spring with the Green and Gold Teams competing in some of the games mentioned above, as well as in hurdles and high jumps, etc., and there were various races for children and grown-ups." On April 14, 1912, the day the *Titanic* sank, there was an elaborate Greek Festival with Greek games and costumes. Miss Wilkinson wrote,

> The plan of what should be given, the rehearsals, the costumes, the transportation of the whole school population, little as well as big, demanded endless decisions. In those modest days, it was at first proposed that every child should wear white stockings, but fortunately the decision was reversed so that the children were to go truly Greek, with bare legs. But with the uncertainty of spring, a wind from the North Pole blew across Hartsdale, so that each room teacher was busy wrapping sweaters round her children, dressed in cheesecloth, unwrapping them for their part in the per-

Tug of War: Greek Games at Hartsdale, circa 1915

formance, and re-wrapping them in garments no Greek ever wore. Through it all Miss Chapin repeated that it would be an admirable advertisement for the school, as indeed it was, for all sorts of people drove out in touring cars and chiffon veils to see our Greek Festival, and no children caught their deaths, thanks entirely to the room teachers.

Later, a fall Field Day was added. On November 23, 1918, there was a dogfight between the Green and Gold canine mascots at roll call, but the rest of the day passed peacefully. The Golds added a sharp touch to their athletic attire by wearing one gold and one black stocking.

A less popular athletic tradition was Demonstration Day at the YMCA at Fiftieth Street and Tenth Avenue and later at the Y on Lexington Avenue at Fifty-third Street. Here the girls were given the opportunity to show their parents all they had learned in gymnastics at school. Gymnastics as the core of Chapin's physical education program gradually gave way to games and dancing, but the 1918 *Wheel* credits the gymnastic training with being of great value to alumnae in the work of Miss Chapin's Alumnae Military Drill Unit.

The school's physical education program was designed to build and maintain good health. Every girl was required to come back to school one afternoon a week for games. In 1924 New York State required an hour of gymnastic drill and marching each week as well as three hours of recreation under "home supervision." The gymnasium was stocked with equipment and apparatus "for the proper development of growing girls." The girls' reactions were mixed. One wrote how she hated gym. "To get all dressed up in black stockings and bloomers and then have to jump over things, hang from ladders and things in the ceiling" was not to her liking. Another loved gym. "You went down the ladder by swinging from side to side. I thought that was terribly exciting."

Commencement ceremonies at the school have varied little since Miss Chapin's day. No academic awards are given. The class stands together for the last time, united, with no differentiations made. The girls always have worn white dresses, sometimes long and sometimes short, and until recently there has been a Commencement dinner given by the headmistress. "Miss Chapin gave a dinner at her house, and every girl was expected to stand up and speak. Miss Chapin would ask each girl to complete a written questionnaire about her thoughts and ambitions. But these were so confidential that the girls never saw their classmates' answers."

Miss Chapin also wrote a poem for each of her graduates. Her poems for two Self-Government presidents follow. First, to Alma de Gersdorff Morgan '15:

> *A health to Alma, full of hopes and fears*
> *Who learned to dare although she feared to lose*
> *Till fears forgotten, in the passing years —*
> *She won, she wins, she leads us as we choose*
> *Our love goes with her to the world outside*
> *Where further hopeful lessons shall be taught her*
> *And Alma Mater points with loving pride*
> *And true rejoicing at her Alma Daughter.*

The first formal Commencement: the Class of 1913

And to Anne Morrow Lindbergh '24:

> *You have led us as a general*
> *Through our troubles and our pleasures*
> *Never tiring of the task that helped us all,*
> *We have stored away forever*
> *In our box of hidden treasures*
> *Thoughts of Anne that forever we'll recall.*

In Miss Stringfellow's time, the poems were written and read aloud by Miss Wilkinson at the class dinner.

Summer work and the summer reading list, on which the girls were marked, were instituted so that during vacation they would not forget what they had learned during the school year. The girls were expected

The Class of 1993 at Commencement

to do thirty hours of "useful work" as well as to memorize four poems, read four books and write book reports. In addition, they were to do a certain number of arithmetic problems, and to collect butterflies, press wildflowers or complete some other science project. The handsomest projects were put on the honors table at the Parents' Tea for Summer Work, which was given in the fall. "As time wore on," reported Adele Ely, teacher of mathematics in the Lower and Middle Schools for many years, "there were more and more complaints over the unfairness of the platform display of work as much of it had been done by a governess or parent." The summer reading list, revised many times, is still in existence. One alumna, Mary Elizabeth Dyer de Garis '24, called it "the most significant feature" of her Chapin education, as it led her to a lifetime of browsing around libraries.

The Upper School Student Self-Government system, introduced by Miss Chapin in 1909, and run by the girls with her supervision, was a

"IN A KINGDOM OF OUR OWN"
Self-Government commentary, *The Wheel*, December 1921

tradition that reflected the values she wished so ardently to teach her students. At her suggestion, the students wrote their own constitution, which was borrowed more than ten years later by the Horace Mann School as a model for its student government. The monthly meetings of the Advisory Council, made up of the officers of Self-Government and of other school organizations, were especially valuable exercises. One alumna recalled, "When we had Advisory Council meetings, Miss Chapin taught us how to think and how to solve problems and to see the other person's point of view."

In 1926 Miss Wilkinson wrote that the Advisory Council "has assumed so many duties, and wishes to take on so many more that soon it will become as busy as the United States Cabinet and will have to have all-day sessions with an hour out for lunch! For breaking rules now a girl receives a mark, with the accompanying disgrace of having this posted on the bulletin board. A certain number of marks deprives a girl of certain privileges."

There were many rules for which girls received demerits. Uniforms had to be in order. Chewing gum was forbidden. No lipstick or nail polish was allowed. Not asking permission for various things was an offense, as was taking two steps at a time on the stairs. Girls had to march in lines from class to class until they were in Fifth Class. Bible verses had to be memorized. Defacing the building carried a penalty of three marks; talking or running on the stairs, one mark; talking after recess bell, one mark; disorder in the library, two marks; disorder before singing, News, general exercises, gymnasium, after Prayers and while waiting to enter the Assembly Room, two marks. One mark was the penalty for disorder in the Study Room when no teacher was present, for throwing paper on the floor or in desks, or for representatives not attending committee meetings. Girls were not to swing their arms while walking, but to keep them quietly at their sides; they were also told to walk with toes pointed straight ahead, not out. After a student received a certain number of marks, she had to appear before the Advisory Council for a disciplinary hearing.

A common punishment was being banished from Club or participation in a play. More serious offenses resulted in expulsion from the Athletic Association for a week. Often one's misconduct was announced in Prayers. Suspension from the library was considered appropriate punishment for those who were disorderly there. After still more miscon-duct, the miscreant might have to recite the rules of Self-Government either to the Advisory Council or to Miss Chapin, Miss Fairfax and the Upper School. The worst punishment was to be forbidden to wear the uniform.

One case of misconduct that was never brought up before the Advisory Council concerned young Sophie Duer. According to Georgina Wells Van Rensselaer '20, "My cousin Sophie was studying in the library, which featured an exhibition of paintings. A gentleman, a friend of Miss Bailey's, came in, and he put his hands behind his back with his hat in his hands and walked around the table examining the pictures. Well, that was too much for Sophie. She wrote a little note saying, 'you are the apple of my eye,' and dropped it in his hat. Later the gentleman found the note and delivered it to Miss Chapin, and Miss Chapin almost had a fit. She called Sophie into her office and told her she was the most depraved girl in the world to do such a thing. Sophie came out crying."

An important offshoot of Self-Government, one that dominated the minutes for years, was the establishment in 1918 of the Pound for lost articles. From the beginning this was a moneymaking proposition. "When there is a congestion of articles which have been left unclaimed for some time, a sale is held at which the different pieces of property are sold for ten cents each." In addition the girls had to pay a fee to retrieve their own possessions. An editorial in *The Wheel* in 1920 admonished the girls, "The fact that a 'pound' is necessary at all shows a shiftlessness in regard to our belongings."

In 1922 Miss Chapin, despairing of the general collapse in responsible behavior reflected in the increase of lost articles and outbreaks of mischief, created the post of public service officer. These officers would offer "helpful suggestions in such matters as traffic regulations, order at lunch and after recess, and act as a positive influence in matters of general politeness and courtesy."

Elizabeth Gay Pierce '25 summed up Chapin's mission: "We were taught ethics. That was the most significant feature." Honesty was essential. When asked by a student if it were ever justifiable to tell a lie, Miss Chapin replied, "Louise, I'm a great many years older than you are, and I have never found anything that would equal the truth." Although good study habits and academic excellence were hallmarks of the new school, courtesy and consideration for others came first. Miss Chapin herself practiced the most perfect tact. She was thoughtful and took the girls'

"So, on the whole, there is very little to say about self-government, and this is also the best that could be said about it. For self-government, like the government of a country, is happiest without a history." *The Wheel*, May 1934

comments seriously. When a student said she wasn't so sure about eternal life, about living forever and not being able to stop, Miss Chapin commented, "a great many other people in the history of the world have thought what you are saying now," and they talked about it.

Money was rarely discussed. Although there was a disparity of wealth among their families, the girls neither knew nor cared. It was not polite to talk about it. As one alumna recalled, "Miss Chapin cared very much about our being simple and moral.... High ideals were appreciated."

Alumnae often commented on the sense of self-confidence Chapin gave them. These comments are typical: "The whole rich background of all the classics that we read, the Greek and the Latin, made an enormous difference. It made you self-confident, because you knew you could do this, that and the other. You were as good as the boys." Yet, true to her time, one of Miss Chapin's favorite pieces of advice was, "Girls, you won't ever make the mistake, will you, of putting a career before a happy marriage?"

In addition to self-confidence, courtesy and high standards, a sense of civic duty was instilled in the girls. Miss Stringfellow commented that "Miss Chapin believed women should be educated for useful citizenship and take a part in community affairs whether they went to college or not." When May Swords Hoppin '26 was asked what had served her best from her Chapin education, she replied, "A sense of public responsibility. We were privileged, and therefore we owed. Because you had advantages, you gave back." Georgina Wells Van Rensselaer had a perfect attendance record, of which she was extremely proud, and she balked at missing school to unveil a portrait of her great-grandfather, who had been a federal court judge in New York. Miss Chapin said, "It is your civic duty to go down there and unveil the portrait." And so Georgina went.

Miss Chapin's outlook on social problems was advanced for the times, and she shared her views with the students. She expected them to take an interest in current civic and world affairs. Miss Chapin was also a feminist and a suffragette. She stressed the dignity of womanhood and made her students proud of being women. She encouraged in them the feeling that they could climb mountains and conquer the world. "The hand that rocks the cradle should never be seen at the polls" was not a Chapin maxim. Around 1915 Miss Stringfellow joined Miss Chapin in a parade for women's suffrage. Miss Chapin said she could not march up Fifth Avenue without a band, so she paid for one to lead the private schools and colleges section of the parade. A number of students and faculty marched with her.

Suffragette parade, circa 1915

Miss Spence was one of many of Miss Chapin's acquaintances who did not approve. According to Miss Stringfellow, she wrote Miss Chapin: "I'm amazed that you would march in a parade. That's very bad for your school." Miss Chapin wrote back: "I did not march as the Headmistress of The Chapin School. I marched as Maria Bowen Chapin, and I reserve the right to express myself in any way I want." Later she went to Washington as a member of a New York contingent to talk with President Wilson on the rights of women.

Miss Stringfellow was also criticized for taking part in the march. Her aunt was so furious that she left New York. Miss Stringfellow remembered her saying that "she couldn't bear to think of anybody related to her in the parade. I had the most scathing letter from my mother because they took pictures of us. We were a very gay group because of the band and everybody took our picture. And it was shown on the screen at Tuscaloosa, Alabama, and someone recognized me. Well, to have a Stringfellow marching up Fifth Avenue was more than mother could take!"

CHAPTER THREE

TIME FOR CHANGE

It is a wonderful school with an excellent building, marvelous girls, and a transcendent faculty, and the only detail that is intolerable is that the bus should drive around the city to collect and deposit the pupils, marked Chapin School LIMITED.... We are not limited in any way: our possibilities are unlimited, as they always have been and always will be.

KATHARINE MAY WILKINSON
TEACHER OF HISTORY, 1904–1952

*I*n 1917, the fateful year America entered World War I, the first issue of *The Wheel* was published. The student editorial states its aim: "to represent the literary activity in the school by stories, poems and essays written by the girls; and to furnish a report on the life of the school in the notes of the alumnae, Club and Athletic Association."

The early editorials read like sermons, reflecting creditably on Miss Chapin's moral influence. They exhort Chapin students to serve their community, to use good judgment, to think matters through and to change school activities where change is within their power if they think it would be beneficial. Girls are frequently chastised for being careless and thoughtless. "Very few people are born honest," declares one early opinion piece. "One must exercise unceasing effort and self-

Field hockey, 1926

Come to
RED CROSS.
and sew.

Drawing from *The Wheel*, February 1919: The Red Cross Auxiliary 242 at Chapin contributed children's garments as well as dressings and knitted articles.

discipline in order to become thoroughly honorable. If we are heedless now and think that absolute rectitude is not necessary in small school matters, we shall find it so much the more difficult to be quite upright in the larger activities of later life."

As the horrors of the war drew closer, *The Wheel* shook Chapin students from their schoolgirl cocoons. "This is a period so stirring and so tremendously significant that our indifference to the affairs of the world is no less than criminal. It is thus our manifest duty to devote a part of our spare time to reading newspapers and current reviews."

Beyond the editorial page, *The Wheel*'s stories, essays and poems of this period sound less like Miss Chapin and more like teenage girls. Interspersed among romances and melodramas, ghost stories and whimsies with titles such as "The Life History of a Bad Nickle" and "The Tale of Princess Gwendolyn" are articles of startling seriousness, such as "A Summary of the Industrial Revolution and Its Results in England" and "William Morris in Relation to Art." Several stories deal with the war. One very imaginative one is about a silent ship, manned by ghosts and captained by Lord Nelson, which quietly goes about its business of shelling and sinking German submarines. Another, "Sadie," tells the tragic story of a switchboard operator who was blown up while working in a munitions factory. Many selections deal with myths and the supernatural.

In an article for *The Wheel* entitled "The Effect of the War upon Our School," Eleanor Marshall Capen '19 wrote, "Most noticeable were the posters, pamphlets and booths for Liberty Loans or the Red Cross Drive in the front hall. At the head of the stairs stood a sketch of President Wilson summoning us to join the Red Cross." In Class Twelve, geography was modified and a civics course introduced. Gymnasium work became more military, and semaphoring was taught on the playground.

Katharine Walker MacKenty remembered several Chapin alumnae who went abroad, rented large houses in France or Belgium and provided nursing care for the injured. President N. Monsserran of the Russian Red Cross awarded Doris Matthews '13, a Red Cross worker, a magnificent document in appreciation for her aid to Russian refugees. In part, it states, "The noble way in which you have come forward, understood us, and helped us to bear our adversity will never be forgotten." Baron P. Mengden wrote to Doris, "It is with great sorrow that we tell you good-bye. You, as a gentle young lady with your sensitive and delicate soul, have brought so much warmth and tenderness in our tormented minds, that our gratitude to you is endless and will remain always in our hearts till the end of our lives."

Anti-German feeling ran high among the parents, faculty and students, and because of this, Miss Chapin had to make a particularly courageous decision in regard to her German teacher, Anna Bernkopf, whose classes were being boycotted. Fräulein Bernkopf came to school every day for four years to an empty classroom. "Miss Chapin would not give in to the pressure [to discontinue German classes] because she knew she was right."

War news was often the subject of talks at Prayers and News. "Miss Chapin rang the assembly bell unexpectedly during classes one day in 1917 and announced to the surprised students that the Czar of Russia had been overthrown; she tearfully dismissed the school early." Margaret Brett Tenney '25 recalled, "On November 11, 1918, at 11:00 A.M., Miss Chapin summoned us to assembly. There she told us, 'The war is over!'" The girls sang "America the Beautiful," which moved Miss Chapin greatly. "We could hear the tumult outside on the streets. After a brief ceremony, for no one could speak, she rang the bell. 'School dismissed!' We poured into a New York we would not see again, nor ever forget, for its joy and warmth."

Doris Matthews '13 in her Red Cross uniform

Acknowledging Armistice Day, the Chapin students attended a memorial service at the Cathedral of St. John the Divine, as reported in *The Wheel.* "Everyone of us entered solemnly, and quietly took the place assigned to her. Not once during the service did our attention waver. If only we could treat our morning prayers with like seriousness. We should, moreover, learn our Bible verses, and not regard them as an irksome task."

When the war ended, *Wheel* editorials urged the girls to profit by the lessons of economy, self-denial and cooperation they had learned during the conflict. War had led them to a broader view of life. "If formerly we were absorbed only in our own local affairs, we have now become aware of larger, more abiding aims." Miss Chapin wanted her girls to be involved in serious issues and to think for themselves. During the November 1920 political campaign, Chapin held a straw poll, in which the girls voted formally and with seriousness for the presidential candidates.

Gradually the girls were attracted to more frivolous peacetime activities. They stopped attending the meetings of the school's Red Cross Auxiliary 242. Parties became more lavish; costume balls and extravagant coming-out parties were all the rage. Georgina Wells Van Rensselaer wrote, "My godfather, Harris Fahnestock, gave my coming-out party at his house just off Fifth Avenue and 65th Street. I wore a lovely silver and white dress, with a wreath of rosebuds from shoulder to waist. A lame friend, who sat and counted how many men cut in on me as I circled the ballroom, said I had 40 cut-ins on the way around."

Her students' need for a channel for their rambunctious energies, not to mention her own love of drama, prompted Miss Chapin to start the Dramatic Club for Upper School girls in 1920. Jane Wyatt Ward '28, who went on to become a successful professional actress, was a president of the club. "I had some wonderful parts," she recalled. "I played Joan of Arc. My best part was playing Shylock." In 1923 a school orchestra was formed, and in the following year, the Choral Club.

New teachers were added to the faculty, several of them destined to become Chapin legends. Chapin's greatly loved writing teacher, Grace Morris Affleck, came in 1926. She was a professional illustrator as well as a teacher, and "our first understanding of form, of letter writing, of neatness, and of the beauty of the written word, not to mention the importance of spelling, came from her patient and warm teaching. Miss Affleck opened a beautiful new world to us." Another student wrote, "She taught us all to write. She made everybody have nice round legible handwriting. We were never taught to connect our letters. You can recognize Chapin handwriting on any envelope, anywhere."

Miss Affleck's specialty was illumination and manuscript writing. One girl remembered, "No one ever had quite her style, and I don't mean just the beautiful lettering of which I still cherish examples. It was her personal style, a composite of good humor and tolerance and a sharp eye. She had a way of swinging into the room, a buoyant form, as confident as Queen Victoria, and enjoying herself twice as much as ever Queen Victoria did."

Miss Affleck's spelling rules were also memorable. Generations of girls are still reciting her famous sentence for remembering the exceptions to the *i* before *e* rule: "Neither of the leisured foreigners seized their heifers on the weird heights."

The Alumnae Association, whose members had worked hard during the war, now turned their hand to helping children in the city. They

Members of the Alumnae Health Bureau, 1927

teamed up with the Grosvenor Neighborhood House in Turtle Bay to form the Chapin Alumnae Health Bureau. In 1923 they held a Babies' Clinic every Tuesday afternoon, as well as a Children's Clinic, attended by a doctor and a social worker. They also started a health club for undernourished children, where they taught the children about good nutrition, and held games three afternoons a week to improve the posture and general physical condition of the children. One alumna wrote, "It was not an easy task to find just the right sort of work: interesting work that could be carried on by a limited number of volunteers, without much experience—that would not incur too heavy financial responsibility, and that offered real possibility of broad development and service."

Miss Chapin was recognized as a leading educator. She instituted the Scholarship Foundation to aid girls and women in New York City "to obtain and carry on their education in any department, literary, professional, industrial, artistic or vocational…and to maintain and award scholarships to girls and women." She was one of the founders of the Head Mistresses Association of the East, serving as its president from 1920 to 1924. She encouraged her teachers to study the latest techniques in education and to use them in school. When the renowned early childhood educator Dr. Maria Montessori came to the United States, Miss Chapin insisted that the entire Lower School faculty go to hear her speak. Miss Stringfellow and one other teacher were required to take classes on the Montessori system. Miss Stringfellow recalled, "Whatever came along we had to know about it, whether we incorporated it or not. She was always looking into the future."

Yet Miss Chapin also held firmly to the ideals of education that she believed had stood the test of time. In her 1925 letter to the alumnae of Miss Abbott's School she wrote, "It is evident that we are too conservative to satisfy the extreme modernists, and far too radical, too much given to experiment, to please those who think 'education is not what it once was.' It is true that we have never printed our course of study because we make so many changes that it would too soon be out of date. Yet we believe in drill and drudgery as firmly as we do in initiative and self-expression."

The following excerpt from a speech Miss Chapin gave at the first meeting of the Baltimore Parents League illustrates her gift for rhetoric:

> Our generation cannot do the work of the next. We may not toil in the vineyard of the future, but we must endeavor to prepare the laborers. Our task is plainly set before us. It will take many generations still to make the world an ideal place for our descendants to live in, but this one thing we must attempt. We must help our boys and girls to become men and women strong enough and sane enough to do their own part to meet and improve their own conditions.
>
> We have faith that they will see ways out of the labyrinths in which we have wandered helplessly. How could we, parents and teachers, find the courage to fight so persistently, and the patience to work so untiringly, to set these little ones free if we did not believe that even where we have failed they may…nay *will* succeed.

In the 1920s Miss Chapin began to take steps to ensure that her school would survive her. She wrote that she and Miss Fairfax hoped "that our work has in it some vital qualities that entitle it to live after us." Incorporation was the answer, but that could not be done in New York State if a school made a profit for its owners. Miss Chapin solved the problem by forming two corporations, one to hold the real estate and the other to own the school. The second would rent the buildings from the first.

Incorporation was made possible by the immediate generosity of members of the Chapin family, followed by numerous subscribing alumnae and others. Miss Chapin's and Miss Fairfax's projected salaries were less than the income they had been receiving from the school, but they were willing to accept the reduction as long as the partial or total free tuition that they had been accustomed to giving certain children might be maintained.

At a special meeting of the proposed Board of Trustees on May 6, 1925, the name of the corporation that was responsible for running the school was resolved to be Miss Chapin's School, Ltd. A second corporation—the 32 East Fifty-seventh Street Corporation—was formed to oversee the school's property. The first meeting of its Board of Directors was held May 28, 1925, at which the certificate of incorporation was approved, bylaws adopted, officers elected and stock issued to the original subscribers.

The first meeting of the Board of Trustees of Miss Chapin's School, Ltd., was held on October 14, 1925. The charter members of the Board were: Miss Chapin and Miss Fairfax (ex officio); Mrs. Dwight W. Morrow, president; Mrs. Harold I. Pratt, vice-president; Earle Bailie, treasurer; Frederic W. Allen; Mrs. Courtlandt D. Barnes; Lansing P. Reed; George Emlen Roosevelt; Roberts Walker; and Aileen Osborn Webb '10.

As the corporations were being organized, the school was outgrowing its buildings, and the neighborhood was becoming increasingly noisy. Fifty-seventh Street was congested with traffic and coarsened by commerce. Miss Chapin began to look for a better location.

From the day Miss Chapin and Miss Fairfax had first discussed incorporating the school, Miss Chapin had envisioned a new building where there would be fresh and invigorating air, abundant

The traffic congestion on Fifty-seventh Street in 1927

sunshine and ample room for the girls to exercise and play games. Astute as ever, Miss Chapin was able to see past the dilapidated tenements and warehouses that in 1920 cast their dismal shadows on the waterfront property she had chosen for the new building, an expanse of land by the East River near Gracie Mansion. One trustee would later recall the doubts of his colleagues, commenting, "I assure you when East End Avenue was first described to us it seemed like a faraway land, a voice from an unknown country." However, Miss Chapin prevailed, and with the Board's approval, engaged the architectural firm of Delano & Aldrich to design the building. The cost was to be about fifty cents per cubic foot, making the total expense in the vicinity of $375,000.

Basketball at Hartsdale, 1921–22

On November 8, 1926, Miss Chapin signed a letter to "The Holders of Common Stock and Thirty Year Sinking Fund Second Mortgage Five Per Cent Gold Bonds of 32 East 57th Street":

It is a great pleasure to be able to announce to the patrons and friends of Miss Chapin's School Limited that a site has been found and purchased on which it will be possible to erect such a new school building as we all desire. The lot is situated on Carl Schurz Park, on the northwest corner of 84th Street and East End Avenue and 148 feet on 84th Street.

The land is situated so that the building will have the light and sunshine so hard to find. The fact that East End Avenue is only ten blocks long will keep it from becoming a thoroughfare and ensure us as much quiet as can be found anywhere in New York. While the land was expensive, it was cheaper than in other localities, and therefore a property was secured with space enough for a satisfactory building, not too many stories high, as well as an excellent yard for games. Last but not least, the beautiful view of the river and sky should add something of inestimable value to the gifts the school may offer.

It is necessary that the building should be adequately equipped. It is desirable that it should keep the atmosphere of simplicity. It is to be hoped that it may be beautiful.

A fund of $500,000 was considered essential to "place the school in a position to do the work that its friends wish it to do." The Building Fund, the school's first capital fund drive, was primarily run by trustees Earle Bailie and Aileen Osborn Webb. A pamphlet, outlining the reasons for the new buildings and the necessity of a building fund, was sent to parents and alumnae. "In seeking a site for the new school," it stated, "the ideal which was held in mind was a plot large enough to hold a dignified and commodious building with light, air and quiet environment."

As the final year on Fifty-seventh Street drew to a close, nostalgia for old ways was outweighed by Miss Chapin's anticipation of the new. Years later, Miss Wilkinson wrote, "At teachers' meetings in the face of new problems, the assertion would be made, 'We've always done it this way,' to which Miss Chapin would reply, 'Then it's probably time we made a change!'"

The new school: 100 East End Avenue, by Delano & Aldrich

Contributions poured in. A big thermometer was placed in the hall of the Fifty-seventh Street school, and the girls watched with excitement as the red line rose steadily to its goal. Later, once the school had moved to 100 East End Avenue, the trustees discovered that Miss Chapin had chosen more wisely than they knew, for property values had already begun to rise.

Miss Chapin knew, however, that a beautiful school building would be only a shell without a sustaining philosophy within its walls. The stone and brick, in the words of Miss Wilkinson, "must be transmuted by the spirit in the experience of the beholder into a finer sense of values, a deeper meaning of work, and responsibility and of love of mankind."

A significant statement by the Right Reverend William Lawrence, bishop of Massachusetts, in the pamphlet outlining the reasons for the new building, also expresses the founder's vision for her school: "A school composed of the children of the rich soon becomes a school such as the rich do not want to send their children to. They will be poorly educated to meet life; for next to able and intelligent teachers, able and intellectual children from different groups are essential to a good school.... The segregation of any one class is fatal to the rounded education of that class."

☙

The academic year of 1928–1929 got off to a good start with the October 31 dedication exercises for the new building at 100 East End Avenue. Dean Virginia C. Gildersleeve of Barnard College gave a speech in which she remarked, "This is a good school. I have long thought of it as one of the pillars of women's education in New York City, a firm foundation on which to build the higher structure of college and university." Dean Gildersleeve's speech drew inspiration from the "cosmic ray" theory of Dr. Robert Millikan. She likened the school to the sun, self-perpetuating and immortal, constantly radiating forth light, energy and life. "The sun of the school does not burn itself out, for constantly the cosmic rays come back to it from space in the strength and support and new spirit from its thousands of graduates.... We may picture the Chapin School as we look forward into the years to come, a glowing star, perpetually reborn, radiating forth always from these halls new energy, new life, new light."

Mrs. Harold I. Pratt, as president of the Board of Trustees, also spoke, and she gave Miss Fairfax particular credit for her contribution to the new building. "This is a truly cooperative building, for Miss Fairfax consulted the head of each department, and passed on to Mr. Aldrich their suggestions, even to the most minute measurements. It is no exaggeration to say that the simplicity of administration of this building is due to the foresight and thought of Miss Fairfax upon the many conveniences which have made it the success it is."

Vita glass was used in the east and south windows so that the ultraviolet rays of the sun, now considered so dangerous, would reach the girls. The lunchroom was put on the sunny fifth floor for the same reason. The walls of the new building were painted light green, which was considered the proper color to study by. A room with a particularly glorious view was allotted to the First Class, because Miss Chapin thought little children should be able to see the river. Miss Stringfellow later commented that Miss Chapin had wanted the school to be low in height: "She wanted the girls to mix in traveling through the building." Miss Fairfax had been so firm about having a greenhouse that she paid for it herself, and Margaret Henderson Bailie planted trees outside the building. The gracefully carved stone drinking fountain in the front hall near the gymnasium was given by Miss Spence's School.

When the school was moved to East End Avenue the fifth-floor lunchroom provided a substantial midday meal, served family style, for faculty and students. Faculty were given a choice of a hot lunch or a sandwich. The two favorite meals were macaroni and cheese and bone-less leg of lamb with mint jelly, served with a bread, onion and celery stuffing. Other popular items were meat loaf, chicken à la king, baked ham, apple crisp with hard sauce, prune whip and the traditional Chapin brownies.

Students responded enthusiastically to the new building, but a passage from the February 1929 *Wheel* shows there was nostalgia for the old.

We liked the old School. We were perfectly contented with the patched stone front and with the crooked cracks in the yellow wall. They had a comforting and a friendly look. And so, we thought suspiciously of change. Even for the first week or two in the New Building, we were not quite sure what to think. Dazed and bewildered, we explored.

Evidently Fifty-seventh Street and Madison Avenue is not Eighty-fourth Street and East End Avenue. One is a wide-streeted mixture of creaking trolley cars and sputtering automobiles, the other is a wide-streeted stretch by a park and a river.... As yet, we are not used to seeing the School as a red brick building. We regard it impersonally, but we can not help admiring it, as a whole. On the inside, however, we think in detail.... We can walk around in the halls and on the staircases, uncramped. We can run around in the yard, and on the roof, unrestrained by contacts with walls. A School, also, is usually connected with thinking, and so we can also think, free from the smallness of classrooms, close air and bad light.

A student wrote of the new building, "I loved the space. The Assembly Room and Gym were three times as big as on 57th Street. When we got to our sixth-grade classroom we all were glued to the window. Miss Stringfellow stood and discussed everything we saw."

The portraits of Miss Chapin and Miss Fairfax by the noted artist Ellen Emmett Rand were commissioned at the time of the move to East End Avenue and partially underwritten by the Alumnae Association. They have always hung in the original library of the school, later known as the Berendsen Room. This library instantly became a favorite room. An editorial in *The Wheel* describes "a long room. Outside swarms a world of activity, but inside everything is still.... The deep mulberry of the carpet, the bright figured curtains, the rich brown woodwork and the gay lampshades all blend together softly. Portraits of Miss Chapin and Miss Fairfax gaze down upon the room. Sunlight streams in through the windows making oblongs of light mulberry on the dark carpet. The dust motes drift gently through the light. We yield to the magic spell."

While East End Avenue was still on its way to becoming a desirable location, Chapin parents were worrying over how to get their daughters to school. In the late 1920s the neighborhood around Chapin was largely untamed; there were only small houses and the streets were of cobblestone. As one alumna commented, "We'd none of us ever been east of Lexington before the school was opened and it was a terrible shock." As a remedy, 105 East Eightieth Street was leased for a bus terminal and meeting place. It was known as the Dump because fathers would "dump" their daughters outside of the house prior to their being shuttled to the school. "Mam'selle [the governess] would take us to the brownstone. If it rained we could wait inside." The second and third floors of the premises were rented to two ladies, one a teacher at the school. When the lease on the building expired in 1931, Miss Fairfax recommended that it not be renewed and that instead Chapin charter a double-decker Fifth Avenue bus to transport the girls to school. In 1953 the school switched to the Campus Coach Company.

Bookplate, The Chapin School Library, 1928–1972

Shortly before the school moved to East End Avenue, Miss Chapin had been involved in negotiations for a new Saturday playground. In 1927 she reported that the Scarborough School in Scarborough, New York, was willing to rent its playing fields on Saturdays throughout the school year. In November of 1929 the Board revealed that the Scarborough School had agreed to build special fields for Chapin's use on a tenyear basis with a lease of $2,800 a year. Scarborough was a boarding school whose students went home on weekends; thus the main building was also rented to Chapin for weekend use.

Several extraordinary women joined the faculty in the early years at East End Avenue. Elsie Bishop arrived in 1928 to assist Miss Fairfax in the mathematics department. She explained things so clearly that even the least mathematical girls finally grasped theorems and formulas. Joanna Bailie Gunderson said that "Miss Bishop did not seem beautiful to me at the time but now I see her loveliness. She showed great kindness and patience to me." Another student remembered helping a friend with her homework every night. The friend went to Miss Bishop, worried that perhaps she was cheating by receiving so much outside help. "Well," said Miss Bishop, "I certainly can't teach you, and if Barbara can by all means let her do it."

Nesta Lloyd-Thomas came to Chapin in 1929 as a classics teacher. Her sense of humor and her kindness won her pupils' hearts. "My first introduction to the school," said Miss Lloyd-Thomas, "was in Turtle Bay in 1929 when I went to be interviewed. Miss Fairfax rose from a blue sea of examination books wearing a shabby gray sweater and sturdy wool stockings with holes, and with that driven look symptomatic of correcting midyears. A certain brusque charm was nonetheless reassuring, and her directness and 'no nonsense' approach to teaching made Chapin seem a vigorous and interesting school. Miss Chapin herself, in a tidier, more elegant room reflecting her own distinction, looked me over amid a few kind words with the result that though I had arrived in a neutral frame of mind, I left hoping I had passed. When in the fall I first entered 100 East End Avenue, it would never have crossed my mind that I was going to enter it for the rest of my professional life, but its secret charm—its endearing pupils—began to work." Miss Lloyd-Thomas's real love was Greek and, when she could, she moved the girls along very fast. Her top students read the *Iliad* in the original in their second year and were so advanced in Greek when they got to college that one Vassar professor had to figure out a new course for his two Chapin girls, and could barely keep ahead of them.

Marthe Duloux came to Chapin in 1929 expecting to stay for three years but instead remained for twenty-eight. She became head of the French department as well as room teacher for the Eights. Her brief talks to this traditionally unruly class initiated them into the Upper School. One graduate remembered her as a "rather severe-looking woman who made us learn grammar thoroughly. Now I can understand anything and say anything I want in French."

Mary L. Janes also came to Chapin in 1929 as an assistant in the Lower School, and remained for forty-three years. Ruth Proffitt '47 wrote, "She was totally predictable with children. Her mood never

Above, left: Miss Bishop

Above, center: Miss Lloyd-Thomas

Above, right: Mlle. Duloux

Bottom, left: Miss Janes

Bottom, right: Miss Metherall

changed and neither did the atmosphere and tone of her classroom. The children were absolutely sure what to expect when they came to school each day." Miss Janes had a real passion for handwriting and calligraphy, and many a Chapin alumna owes her skill in italic handwriting to her. At Miss Fairfax's instigation, Miss Janes began the study of remedial reading. She understood the importance of the early years of instruction and contributed more than can ever be gauged to the success of two generations of Chapin students. When Miss Janes died in 1982, the trustees paid tribute to her. "She never made a sloppy move. She exuded security, competence and wisdom.... She has that dedication upon which the school rests its reputation as a nurturing institution."

Isabel M. Metherall arrived at Chapin in 1931 and for thirty-two years infused the classics department with drama. Tiny, redheaded and fierce, she was the ideal counterpart to her laconic colleague, Miss Lloyd-Thomas. One pupil remembered, "In class one day I responded, 'How come?' 'How come! How come!' she sputtered, standing up. 'Those words are the worst blight of the English language imaginable.' With that she made me promise in front of the class that I would *never* use 'those words' again."

The crisis of the Great Depression, which affected so much of the world, also had its impact on the Chapin School. College tuition for daughters was the first expense to be cut. A member of the Class of 1931 wrote, "I always wanted to go into medicine, but the Depression hit my family hard. I gave up any thought of going to college or medical school because at that point there was just no money around." Girls spoke of their fathers' salaries being cut in half and of moving with their families into smaller apartments. *Wheel* editorials were somber. "The recent crash has shown us that almost anything may happen and that the wife may have to become the breadwinner for the family. Would it be wiser to omit the choice of Greek or German in the College Division and to substitute a course in stenography and typing?"

Elizabeth Mason Walbridge wrote, "The depression made us aware we might have to have jobs, but, on the other hand, we didn't want to take a job away from someone who truly needed it, so our interests centered on secretarial courses and volunteer work."

In the classroom: members of the Class of 1936

Miss Chapin and Miss Fairfax helped the girls to realize the seriousness of the Depression and also to minimize the importance of money. Adaline Havemeyer Rand '31 had this to say: "Miss Chapin made you think it was beneath anybody with intelligence to worry about money. I saw two girls' families in my class who went from great riches to really rags. That was the first time we began to think in terms of money. You liked the person for what she was."

It became fashionable to downplay extravagance. When the Elevens waited on the alumnae and the Twelves at dinner in 1932 they dressed up in three-dollar paper dresses. Coming-out parties were modest, but still important. To some alumnae looking back, it seems unbelievable how oblivious they were to what was happening at home and in Europe despite a current events class, political science and

News. It must be remembered that they were young, and loved to dance and to have lots of beaux.

Chapin survived the Depression better than most schools. Salaries were never cut and the school was able to "defer or remit entirely tuition payments because of the severe financial distress which various parents are now having." Miss Fairfax asked for authority to be easy in collecting bills and to forgive the same entirely when it seemed necessary.

Although the creation had strength enough to survive the Depression, the creator did not. After 1928 Miss Chapin no longer tried to teach every grade, but continued with world history in the Fourth Class, Shakespeare in the Eighth and Bible in the Upper School. Having performed the labors of Hercules to move the school into its beautiful new building by the river, she seemed tired. In 1931 she acknowledged that she was ill. Finally, at a meeting of the Board of Trustees on Monday, May 9, 1932, she tendered her resignation as headmistress of the school, effective September 30. Upon the vote of the Board, her wish was granted, and she was released from her contract with the school with the following understanding: "That she accept a position designated as Founder of the School, remain a member of the Board of Trustees and be available for counsel whenever possible. That as far as her time and health permit, she will conduct the Morning Prayers of the School and also will hold a series of Reading Hours with the Graduating Class."

In the same board meeting, Miss Stringfellow was named joint headmistress of the school with Miss Fairfax and was also made a trustee. She was asked to go abroad during the summer of 1932 to study the Progressive movement in England and in Germany and see how much of its methods Chapin could use, and to attend the International Meeting of Progressive Education.

When Miss Chapin retired and Miss Fairfax and Miss Stringfellow became joint headmistresses, Miss Fairfax put her shyness aside. She came to Field Day and Club, and alternated with Miss Stringfellow in leading Prayers. Upper School girls became particularly fond of her. Students described her as "distinguished" and commented on her "lovely bone structure." They were proud of their headmistress, whom they credited with making Chapin a top school. She paid no attention to the limited expectations New York society set for her girls and gave them the feeling

Miss Fairfax enjoying Field Day

The three headmistresses:
Commencement 1933

that there was nothing they couldn't do if they set their minds to it and worked. An editorial in *The Wheel* of May 1933 reflected the uneasiness the girls felt over the retirement of Miss Chapin. "We dreaded the strangeness of the first year without her.... But our fears were unfounded. Fundamentally, the school is the same. We have not altogether lost sight of Miss Chapin. She has not retired into the fastnesses, as we anticipated. Once a week she presides over us at Prayers. She still conducts her reading class, and she is frequently seen on a tour of inspection, or talking with the girls and teachers."

Of Miss Fairfax and Miss Stringfellow: "The new combination has succeeded magnificently. We have not been revolutionized and the school has gone on smoothly.... On the surface we have changed. But the school which has been founded with toil, inspiration and intelligence, and has been nursed and cultivated into strength and stability—that has not changed."

In February 1934 the name of the school was changed, according to Miss Chapin's expressed wish, to The Chapin School, Ltd. Miss Chapin died of leukemia on March 8, 1934. Funeral services were held at Trinity Episcopal Church at Broadway and Wall Street, conducted by Bishop William T. Manning, who had participated in the school's dedication exercises. Miss Chapin was later buried at Swan Point Cemetery in Providence, Rhode Island. She left a large part of her estate to the school. As the trustees noted at their meeting on April 9, 1934:

Of course, we cannot describe in words the sense of loss we feel. But loss is not the only emotion that affects us. At the first commencement after the incorporation of the School Mrs. Dwight Morrow, President of the Board, announced that the purpose of the incorporation was not to institutionalize the School but just the opposite, to perpetuate Miss Chapin's personality. This we have had as an objective and while we have had the benefit of Miss Chapin's advice we feel we have planned well. Now the test has come and we know we cannot fail for such a personality is immortal. Through all time we feel that her influence for sound scholarship, moral worth and spiritual nobility will always be felt in the field to which she dedicated her life.

Portrait of Mary Cecelia Fairfax by Ellen Emmett Rand, circa 1928

Miss Fairfax became ill soon after Miss Chapin died. She carried on courageously for almost a year, then succumbed to pneumonia on February 28, 1935. The school and the Chapin family turned out en masse for her funeral, conducted by Dr. W. Russell Bowie at Grace Episcopal Church at Broadway and East Tenth Street. Miss Fairfax was buried in Rock Creek Cemetery in Washington, D.C. The trustees paid their tribute to her at their March 1935 meeting. "Miss Fairfax has preserved the standing and character of the School and filled it with Miss Chapin's spirit and her own personality. She combined a very practical devotion to an ideal with a spiritual sweetness that influenced all with whom she came in contact.... Her influence, not only for good, but always for the very best, will continue to be felt from generation to generation."

Elizabeth Forrest Johnson, head of the Baldwin School, wrote of Miss Fairfax for the meeting of the Head Mistresses Association in April 1935: "Of shining integrity, with a direct nature that cut through all sham, with a spirit of generosity and democracy never surpassed, she lived a life of splendid achievement attained in the light of unfaltering ideals and standards.... The cooperation between her and Miss Chapin was a very perfect thing, an integration of such nature that each in living her own life and doing her own distinguished work, rounded out the life and the distinction of the other. It is fitting that they were not long divided."

Miss Fairfax's contribution to the school and her influence on Miss Chapin may never be fully recognized. She was the school's unsung heroine, not only fashioning an academic curriculum that was second to none, but always concerning herself with the well-being of the faculty and staff.

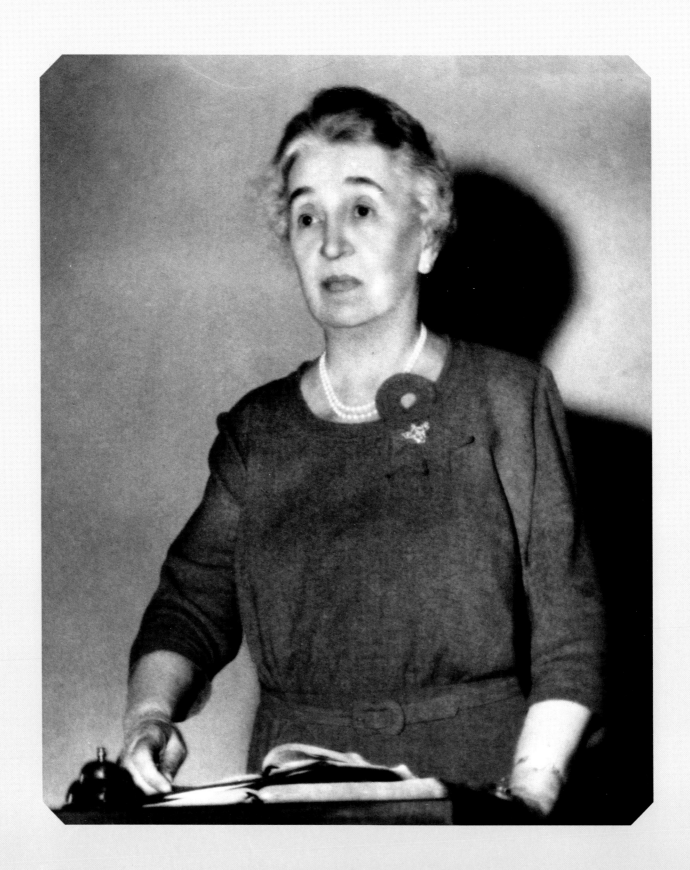

CHAPTER FOUR

THE STRINGFELLOW YEARS

Laughter was her balance wheel.
FRANCES JENNINGS, HEAD OF THE LOWER
AND MIDDLE SCHOOLS, 1934–1963

In 1935 Miss Stringfellow assumed sole command of the school. Over her twenty-six years at Chapin she had become an innovative and highly competent administrator, but she had held Miss Chapin and Miss Fairfax in such high esteem that she had been reluctant to move ahead with the changes she wanted to make while her mentors were still alive.

Frances Jennings, who came to Chapin from Radcliffe in 1934 to teach Class Six, wrote, "Education for Miss Stringfellow was never a solemn enterprise. Laughter was her balance wheel. She realized that humor and learning are compatible. Her every act and word promoted joy in the school. She thought of and ran the school as a family, not as an institution.... Teachers were chosen not only for their scholarship, but for their quality as people. They were always fine human beings who helped create a climate in which children might thrive." She explained that Miss Stringfellow's basic principle was "to provide conditions and create a climate in which every child could grow, to be ever mindful of the derivation of the word educate: *out* + *lead*. We believed in the truth of the ancient Chinese proverb: Teachers open the door, you enter by

Miss Stringfellow at Prayers

Miss Jennings

yourself." On the academic front, Miss Stringfellow made several changes. "One of her first acts as head was to announce her plan for the administration of the school. There would be heads of academic departments and physical education, a Lower School and a Middle School Chairman. I was to be in charge of Class Seven, a connecting link between the Middle and Upper Schools. Two years later, I was appointed head of both Lower and Middle Schools." For her part, Miss Jennings was not only Miss Stringfellow's spokeswoman and champion, but a true "bulwark of the school." When she taught, she looked upon each student as an individual and brought out the best in her. And she shone as an administrator because of her meticulous attention to detail and comprehensive grasp of everything going on in the school.

The mathematics curriculum was revised to meet the new type of comprehensive examinations given by the College Board. The school orchestra was reorganized, and News was revitalized. Well-known lecturers were invited to speak to the girls on current events as well as on exploration, music, literature and drama. On one occasion, "Miss Pearl Buck talked to us on the position of women in China." The lecture series for the year 1945–1946 was impressive. It included "Japan after Defeat" by Lawrence K. Rosiger of the Foreign Policy Association, Edith Hamilton on Greek civilization, and Dr. Wilbur K. Jordan, president of Radcliffe College, on "General Education in a Free Society."

Miss Stringfellow wanted the girls to take advantage of the cultural offerings of the city. For example, attending a Shakespeare play or the opera was not only permitted but encouraged, even on a school night. Miss Stringfellow built up the clubs and fostered other activities both to enrich the lives of her students and to prove to parents that it was not necessary to send their daughters to boarding school.

With children Miss Stringfellow was invariably kind. Susan McIntosh Lloyd '52 remembered, "When I cried inconsolably in first grade, she realized I probably was bewildered by my new school's all female population as I had grown up in a family with four brothers. She must have guessed right because when she sent me down to spend the rest of the morning with Oscar Wagemann [the superintendent] I stopped crying. After a second day of this, she invited me to bring my three-year-old brother to school for about two weeks."

She was free with advice. Anne Keating Jones '39 wrote, "After the graduation dinner she held for the Class of 1939, she told us she enjoyed having us very much and we should remember who we were and where

Members of the Class of 1952 in Class One

we came from and keep our names out of the newspaper." Another well-remembered line was, "Be good listeners."

An early, and in the eyes of the girls, long overdue decision was to change the uniform. In 1936 Miss Stringfellow introduced the new model, designed by Louise Hoadley James '14, a parent and trustee. It consisted of a green A-line skirt and bolero in dark green and a long-sleeved aqua linen blouse with a Peter Pan collar. The younger children wore the same blouse material for their tunics, which no longer featured pleats. Bloomers were still worn for physical education in the Upper School. In the Lower and Middle Schools, bloomers were worn at all times under the tunic, and the girls wore knee socks or white or green short socks. Upper School girls wore thick lisle stockings that did not run. Sensible oxford shoes and a hat completed the outfit. However, the gored skirt with its two false pocket flaps was not designed to flow

"The Start": Louise Hoadley James '14 with briefcase

The Old and the New

Drawing from *The Wheel*
by Linda Gillette Cornet '48

smoothly over adolescent curves, and the bolero jacket added an incongruous Spanish note, jutting out like a shingle over the more generously developed and drooping disconsolately on the less well-endowed. Student reaction was mixed. An editorial from *The Wheel* stated, "This year the changing of the school uniform has outwardly revolutionized our school world. At first most of us, especially the older girls, refused honestly to like the new uniform. We had always worn the old one. We were sentimentally attached to it, and we were going to cling to it with child-like ferocity. But now getting used to seeing it before our eyes, it seems to fit in with the rest of the school; and we take it for granted that it belongs there." The uniform was to stay the same for thirty-five years.

Among Miss Stringfellow's major contributions to the school was the building up of the Alumnae Association, which had become less of a presence in the school after its burst of fund-raising for the new building. The *Alumnae Bulletin* had not been published for several years, and the alumnae were unable to meet their annual pledge of $1,000 to the Scholarship Fund. The March 1935 *Wheel* borrowed a term from President Roosevelt to describe a reorganization of the association: "A New Deal...to create an active interest in the school and in all its activities." The first Alumnae Day, held at the school in the spring of 1935, was a rousing success.

The first Alumnae Luncheon, held at the school on April 21, 1937, and sponsored by five reunion classes, turned the tide. One hundred people attended, including Miss Stringfellow and the Twelfth Class. Katharine Walker MacKenty was proud to report that $1,000 had been given to the school for the Scholarship Fund. The following year 131 attended the luncheon, including sixteen faculty and twenty-four Twelves. A tradition was established that still flourishes.

The alumnae resumed printing the *Alumnae Bulletin* in 1937. In 1944 the school charter was amended, making the president of the Alumnae Association an ex-officio trustee of the school.

In the spring of 1943, the alumnae of Chapin and Brearley opened the Chapin-Brearley Exchange at 72 East End Avenue. The Board

The first Alumnae Luncheon, April 21, 1937

authorized Miss Stringfellow to underwrite the expense of the shop to an amount equal to that assumed by Brearley. Money raised would go to the scholarship funds of the two schools. The Exchange worked on a half-credit/half-cash basis, although all-cash purchases could be made. A customer's credit was established by bringing in outgrown boys' and girls' clothing. The Exchange moved to 429 East Eighty-second Street in 1960 and continued to be an excellent resource for both the Chapin and Brearley families. It closed in 1997, having contributed significantly to both schools.

One of Miss Stringfellow's pet projects in the 1930s was the establishment of the Four Schools Placement Bureau. The bureau, organized by Brearley, Chapin, Nightingale-Bamford and Spence in 1937 and expanded to eleven participating schools by 1946, helped alumnae secure places in business and social service, as well as in educational or artistic fields. In 1951, its heyday over, the bureau merged with the Women's Placement Bureau and the University Personnel Agency on Madison Avenue.

Like Miss Chapin, Miss Stringfellow adored dramatics. Miss Lloyd-Thomas described the Teachers Play, believed to have been instituted by Miss Stringfellow, and given approximately every five years, as "a recurrent horror...fostered and enjoyed by a few who fancied their Thespian talents, but nothing but a penance to me and many others.... It gave great pleasure to the audience." What came to be known as the Faculty Show continued until the early 1980s.

Student health had always been of paramount importance to Miss Chapin and Miss Fairfax, and Miss Stringfellow was even more zealous. In addition to the physical examination, with its emphasis on straight backs, students were inspected carefully for signs of illness after exposure to any contagious disease. Anyone showing the slightest sign of illness was sent home. "There was a very real fear of disease, polio probably most especially. We remember when school was closed for a week because a student had meningitis. There were immunizations for smallpox and diphtheria, but if anyone in the class had mumps, measles, chicken pox or whooping cough, we were obliged to come early to school to have our throats examined and our temperatures taken." In 1937 Miss Stringfellow decided to keep the school nurse on duty all day. Faithful to the philosophies of Miss Yates and Miss Chapin, a gym teacher was instructed to go around the school and look through the portholes in the classroom doors to make sure the girls were sitting up straight.

Miss Stringfellow in costume for the faculty show, *Up on Old Smoky*, 1954

Chapin gained the services of Mary Cheska, a registered nurse from the pediatric division of the Bellevue Hospital, in 1944. Affectionately known as "the mushroom in the basement" because her Bellevue cap looked like a mushroom, she stayed at Chapin for thirty years, "curing cut knees, common colds and schoolgirl sorrows with Bactine, aspirin and much affection." Just looking at Miss Cheska was enough to make a girl feel better. Her warm smile and the twinkle in her eye reassured the students that everything would be fine in a little while.

Miss Cheska

The first issue of the Middle School literary magazine, *The Cog,* was printed in April 1937. The editorial states, "We have named our magazine *The Cog* because many of us feel that the name should have some relation to *The Wheel.* It has been discovered that a cog is one tooth among many teeth at the edge of a large wheel which is fastened onto another wheel. The cogs turning round and round help the other wheel on its course. We felt that this would be a good name for our magazine because it would help *The Wheel* and at the same time be something different." *The Cog* continued to be a wonderful representation of students' creative writing and art.

In 1939 the Dance Club was founded under the inspirational direction of Bonnie Allen, who had come to Chapin to teach dance in 1938. It quickly became one of the most popular afternoon activities. As one alumna put it, "For years we have all refused to dance; then suddenly a Dancing Club appeared and many of our friends were taking part in this formerly taboo art."

Ice-skating, offered through Chapin at Madison Square Garden, became so popular that the girls who took lessons could substitute them for the obligatory games at school. Horseback riding, including polo, was another popular pastime. On Friday afternoons, the girls went to Schrafft's on Seventy-ninth Street or to the automat on Eighty-sixth before going to the movies. Miss Stringfellow also went to the movies at Loew's on Friday afternoons. The girls could hear her laughter throughout the theater. This image of the headmistress corresponds with a wonderful description of Miss Stringfellow by Susanah Bailie Trautman '46: "With her overpowering southern accent and her piercing voice, she could be heard from any part of the six-story school building continuously reminding us to 'be conspicuous by being inconspicuous' and to 'never raise your voice.' Such was the power of her personality that not one of us ever questioned the discrepancy between what she preached and what she practiced."

Miss Stringfellow at Field Day, 1940

A 1936 *Wheel* editorial said, "When we graduate in June, almost every one of us has a definite idea of what we are going to do—the school has trained our minds, given each of us a good foundation, and prepared us for that piece of work in which we are interested." Miss Chapin and Miss Fairfax and now Miss Stringfellow had done their best to train those minds, but it would take World War II to jolt the girls into deeper thoughtfulness just as World War I had the generation before them.

The March 1939 *Wheel* denounced Hitler and Nazism. "The Nazis do not even try to decide anything for themselves, but accept as law every word that falls from the lips of Hitler. Those who have dared to judge for themselves are either exiles or in concentration camps." Student self-government was seen as "part of a free man's answer to Fascism, to Nazism and to the Soviets. It means that we believe that man has a soul. He also has certain rights and the reason to demand them. Liberty, however, is never lawlessness. It is the freedom to live freely and to let our neighbors live freely."

From 1939 on, Chapin students settled down to their studies with renewed zeal and applied to college in greater numbers. Scholastic standards were high. In 1939 the number of girls taking the College Preparatory Course doubled, and in 1940 Miss Stringfellow reported that the dean of Bryn Mawr College could "suggest no improvement in the preparation of our students and only wishes we could send more like them." Their reading scores were above the median of independent schools for the next higher class. Meanwhile, *The Wheel* continued to publish thoughtful and serious stories and poems.

The enormous importance of the war was made clear to even the youngest student when Miss Stringfellow called them into the Assembly Room to hear President Roosevelt's famous "Day of Infamy" speech in December 1941. In early 1942, Miss Stringfellow reported in the *Alumnae Bulletin* on measures being taken at the school because of the war.

During the week following the Japanese attack on Pearl Harbor, the school was organized for air-raid precautions. The warden of the district was asked to come to inspect the building and give suggestions and instructions for procedure in case of an alarm. The girls practised the drill until they did it perfectly. In addition, the transoms of the doors and all inside glass on the corridors chosen for shelter were either taped or removed; a radio was purchased for the office, and first-aid kits and flashlights for the other floors. One of the teachers or older girls who had taken the first-aid course was appointed to direct a station on each floor. Food, fruit juices, bottled water and lollypops have been laid in stock in case the children are confined to the building for several hours or over a meal time. A supply of games has been purchased, and older girls appointed to read to the younger ones or play games with them, and songs have been planned which they can sing without accompaniment. Sand buckets and a spray have been installed on the roof and one of the men on the house-staff stationed on each of the three floors which are to be used as shelters.

The school building was offered to the neighborhood as an air-raid shelter in case of a raid at night or when the school was not in session.

Miss Stringfellow organized campaigns for the sale of Defense Savings Stamps and Bonds. School organizations gave up collecting dues and students were encouraged to buy defense stamps. The girls supported an organization called Young America Wants to Help (perhaps better known as "Bundles for Britain"), which provided clothing for the British war sufferers.

There were many war-related activities in the school. Sewing for the Red Cross consumed Classes Eight, Nine and Ten. In addition to their hand sewing, the girls learned how to stitch on a sewing machine and to press with an electric iron. Children in Classes Two and Three were allowed to stay in school for an afternoon play group twice a week, freeing their mothers for war work. "The Elevens and Twelves were distinguished by bundles of khaki-colored wool that we stuffed in our desks and trailed down the halls as we knitted scarves, woolen helmets and mittens to be sent to troops overseas. In the evenings two elective vocation courses were offered: cooking, taught by Miss Stringfellow, where our pampered generation learned how to make jello, and typing, which was more serious and did prove useful to many of us." Economy was stressed. The girls were taught how to save paper, books and other school supplies. They also had to give up wearing silk stockings. "We hope that Miss Stringfellow notices those of us who are sacrificing glamour in the cause of patriotism and wearing lisle stockings to school. Once despised, lisle has actually become fashionable as a badge of virtue, and we take great pride in wearing the humble fabric." The Class of 1942 chose not to wear long dresses for their commencement. The graduating classes of 1925–1931 had worn short skirts, too, but out of regard for fashion, not economy. Students had become aware of just how precious and fragile democracy could be, and in 1945 extended Self-Government to the Middle School through a Junior Council with its own constitution, patterned after that of the Upper School.

Although the school had been assured in 1942 by the Office of the Petroleum Coordinator for War that it would receive sufficient fuel oil, a shortage of fuel became a crisis in 1943, and it was necessary to install a coal-burning furnace. Bus service was restricted in 1944 to the lower six classes. Club nights were given over to sewing and knitting for the Junior Red Cross, and Middle School girls gave a morning or afternoon study period to the war effort. Alice Nicoll '18, head of the school's physical education department, was the instructor for the Red Cross, and used the large basement room for first-aid courses. The gymnasium was offered for a course in first aid to air-raid wardens during August and September. Chapin was also used as a rationing center for the community, distributing material and issuing ration books to the neighborhood. When help became scarce, older girls offered their services in the lunchroom. When Oscar Wagemann, the resident superintendent, complained to Miss Stringfellow that he had no time to polish the brass, she calmed his ruffled spirits by saying it was quite all right, that he shouldn't worry about it. She said she could easily come to school a little early each day and rub them up a bit, and all would be well. After that the brass knobs were kept beautifully polished and no more was said.

During the war, the curriculum changed. A two-year course in American history replaced the one-year courses in English history and American history for Classes Eleven and Twelve. "The war began to be real to us in Miss Wilkinson's history classes. We began to read the papers carefully, listen to the commentaries of Elmer Davis on the radio and scan magazines for pictures of the War in the Air, the War at Sea and the Battle for Britain. She [Miss Wilkinson] shamed us into beginning to think for ourselves. During the war, each pupil in her class kept a notebook of newspaper clippings following the day-by-day descriptions of events in Russia or China or France. She saw that we attended the newly-formed *Herald Tribune* Forum, where, for the first time outside the classroom, we were exposed to open discussion and debate." The Upper School was divided into three groups for News, so that the girls would have a better opportunity to take part in discussions. More geography was put into the curriculum. Effects of aviation on the human eye, ear, heart and other bodily parts were studied in the Class Nine science course.

Outside the school, the older girls volunteered on Friday afternoons, Saturdays and Sundays in various hospitals in the city as "rubber glove menders, ward aides, escorts or messengers." Chapin students also worked in various branches of the National City Bank during the summer and did farm work on the "Farm for Freedom" project in New York State. Groups of girls took part in conferences at International House on "The United Nations and Racial Cooperation," attended forums at Town Hall on "Youth's Responsibility in the Post-War World," and discussion groups at Friends Seminary and the Ethical Culture School on racial barriers. Two students were selected to take part in the Youth Forum sponsored by the *New York Herald Tribune* on "The World We Want."

Chapin students had developed a strong philanthropic streak. As the war drew to a close, the students sponsored the Marlot School in Holland near The Hague and sent over several boxes of clothing and

Above and Right: Bulb planting in
the mid-1940s

gifts as well as a contribution of $455. The girls received in return a gift of tulip, hyacinth and daffodil bulbs.

War changed the school and the students irrevocably. No one was expected to stay home and simply wait for it to be over, and the possibility of being conscripted into the service was real. According to a May 1942 *Wheel* editorial the question uppermost in the minds of all girls leaving school that year was "Shall I go to college?"

> Too often the impulse of girls is to rush into defense factories or other kinds of war work, believing this to be more important than continuing their education. But this belief, however patriotic, is also short-sighted. True, the government does need women to work in factories; but it also needs women trained in physics and in technical sciences. Right now, perhaps, any able-bodied woman can be useful. But later on, well-educated women, women trained in sciences, in languages, and in economics, will be in even greater demand to help solve the problems of the post-war world.... Now that so few men can get a college education, it is doubly important the girls should receive one.

One Chapin alumna who went into the service was Jane Darlington Irwin '38. She was recruited into the Navy from Vassar on an equal footing with male college graduates and became a supply corps officer in the Waves, "managing money and paying it out." As part of an all-out war effort, the Navy sent her to Radcliffe to take courses at Harvard Business School.

Even after the war some fathers were not in favor of giving their girls a college education, but parents in general became more aware of its importance. As students became more interested in what was happening in the world around them and in going to college for a specific reason, their parents began to take a greater interest in what the school was doing for their daughters in both academic and nonacademic areas. Miss Stringfellow welcomed the changing attitude. She invited parents into the school and expanded the afternoon program. Meetings were held so the mothers of Class Eleven students could hear about colleges their daughters might attend. New academic courses in music, history and political and economic geography strengthened the curriculum. Anticipating the feminist movement of the 1960s, the Twelves were offered a course on the status and work of women.

Miss Stringfellow disapproved of the elaborate parties her young charges were attending. Meetings were held with the mothers of Classes Seven and Eight to plan "more interesting and less expensive parties than the stereotyped ones that seemed fastened upon us by custom or by the promotors of junior cotillions." In the Headmistress's Report for 1946–1947, Miss Stringfellow wrote that parents and alumnae were giving time and interest to the problem of the social life of the young people. They enlisted dance committees to set a fashion for simpler parties at earlier hours. "It is hoped that from simpler beginnings their social life may develop along more natural and wholesome lines." Weekend activities at the school included hobby clubs, workshops of various kinds, games for the teenage girls and museum and field trips under the leadership of teachers.

In 1946 Miss Stringfellow, in cooperation with the Public Education Association, the Parents League of New York and the independent schools of Yorkville, helped found the Yorkville Youth Council, which provided a "program of recreation and wholesome occupation for young people of elementary school age after school hours." Upper School girls joined other volunteers from private and independent schools to help the trained staff members at the recreation areas of P.S. 151 on York Avenue and Ninety-first Street and P.S. 198 on Third Avenue and Ninety-sixth Street. The girls supervised games and arts and crafts for the younger children, formed a newspaper club and assisted in sewing and singing. Miss Stringfellow was gratified by their response. In 1949 she wrote, "Each girl gives two-and-a-half hours a week to the program. This seems a real sacrifice of her free time, for the life of a girl in the Eleventh or Twelfth Class is a very busy one. The girls are very happy in this project and are gaining valuable experience in learning how to manage groups of children. They are learning another fine lesson: that our talents are not given to us for our own enjoyment exclusively, but for the betterment of our community."

The school was entering into what Miss Jennings would call its "Golden Years." Under Miss Stringfellow's leadership, Chapin had become a model for other private schools; indeed in 1948 the headmistress reported, "So many schools have asked for our course of study that we have for the first time published a catalogue." Miss Jennings would write, "Chapin was a model for others because it was unique. We never followed educational fashion or fad; we stayed firmly and faithfully with Miss Chapin's purpose and her idea of sound educational practice, which was good in her day, in our day, and in the present, if only educators have the sense to follow it. By gentle and good-humored application of common sense, Ethel Stringfellow solved all problems."

Miss Stringfellow filled her staff with young college graduates, who had a love of learning, were knowledgeable in their fields and had the desire to share their enthusiasm with others. No sharp lines were drawn, and team teaching was the practice. Heads of departments taught classes in the Lower and Middle Schools. A new teacher would have the extraordinary learning experience of teaching Class Seven English with Miss Morison or a section of history with Miss Wilkinson.

Miss Lloyd-Thomas wrote that "Miss Stringfellow was content to follow traditional patterns with the flexibility that her own innate understanding of the young dictated, securing the best teachers she could and trusting them to maintain high standards. She valued originality, praised and encouraged students and faculty and treated every case as a special case."

Miss Stringfellow's major contributions to the curriculum were in science and music. In 1949 Shelby H. Semmes came to Chapin to be

Miss Stringfellow conferring with Miss Lloyd-Thomas

Miss Semmes

Miss Colie

Mrs. McGregor

Mr. Schrade

head of Chapin's Lower and Middle School science programs. With her keen interest in astronomy and birding, Miss Semmes was a perfect successor to Miss Stewart. The following year, Miss Semmes became head of the entire science department.

With the exception of biology, science had been neglected in the Upper School. Miss Stringfellow addressed the situation by increasing the number of science courses, offering new college preparatory and general courses in chemistry and physics. In 1952 Elizabeth Colie came to Chapin to teach science in the Upper School. The department was expanded to include laboratory courses in chemistry, physics and biology, with hope of offering advanced-placement courses soon. The Board approved Miss Stringfellow's plan to buy additional equipment.

In 1954 Miss Stringfellow reported that the music department had been reorganized. Instrumental music had been introduced in Classes Six, Seven, Eight and Nine, and each girl would receive six weeks of small group instruction in either the violin or the cello. Music lessons were available for the girls on these instruments, and a chamber music orchestra was being formed for them. The overall music program was designed by Ruth McGregor, who taught the cello.

Robert Schrade came to Chapin as a pianist in 1948. He played for the Choral Club and the singing and dance classes. One of the first men to join the faculty, Mr. Schrade remembers an occasional squeal as, after calling "coming through!" he passed through the "Holland Tunnel" in the basement, where the girls had their lockers and changed for dance and physical education. Many alumnae look back on Mr. Schrade's playing as a significant feature of their Chapin education. "He never played silly music. He always played something that made the students feel grown-up and special." Mr. Schrade himself later recalled, "I imparted what I liked to the students. They marched into Prayers to great music, not standard marches. I played thoughtful, reflective music coming in so that the girls would come in quietly, then switched to bright marches when they went out." In his letter to the Class of 1955, who dedicated their yearbook to him, Mr. Schrade wrote, "Music should humbly seek to please, and my greatest desire is that at some moment in our association I may have brought you pleasure."

The caliber of Chapin's choral singing improved greatly. An alumna of 1943 wrote, "What I liked best about Chapin was Choral Club. We got together with a number of independent schools for a concert at Carnegie Hall. I think Robert Shaw was the conductor. There were hundreds of voices." The Choral Club held joint concerts with Yale and Princeton and had interschool sings. In 1954 over two hundred boys and girls from fifteen New York City private schools came to Chapin to sing carols and the simpler portions of the Bach Christmas Oratorio.

Miss Stringfellow believed in the benefits of physical exercise. However, weekend playing time at Scarborough had been cut back, and eventually canceled, because of wartime travel restrictions and expenses. In 1946 she secured the use of the city fields at Randall's Island three days a week during the spring term for softball games and a field in Central Park for hockey three days a week in the fall. Field Day was moved to the Riverdale Country School. During the 1940s Chapin students played games with Rye Country Day School and Nightingale-Bamford, as well as Brearley. Cheerleaders were introduced in 1949.

The girls had used the tennis courts of the Gracie Park Tennis Club immediately to the north of the school since 1934, but by 1944 the courts had deteriorated and the club went out of business. Miss Stringfellow asked the trustees to look into the matter and see what could be done. George Emlen Roosevelt, president of the Board of Trustees, who had originally owned part of the property where 110 East End Avenue now stands, reported that the lot had been sold to a Mr. I. Prussin, "with certain restrictions for the protection of the school, which are still binding." Mr. Prussin offered two alternatives. "He would build a six-story apartment building if the school

Miss Stringfellow at bat, Field Day 1940

Hockey on Randall's Island, 1964

would cancel the present restrictions, or he would build a twelve-story apartment building, with certain specified open space opposite the studio windows of the school to meet our restrictions."

Miss Stringfellow opted for the twelve-story building as long as Mr. Prussin agreed to the following conditions:

> never to build upon that rectangular portion of property which commences at the southwesterly corner of the property and extends easterly for a distance of 102' and southwesterly for a distance of 34'. This request is due to our desire to preserve light and air for the northerly rooms of the Chapin School Building.
>
> We would also require that the service entrance should be on 85th Street and not next to the school on East End Avenue. We would also require that the wall of the court facing on the rectangular plot above referred to be constructed of light-reflecting brick or painted a light color, said paint job to be renewed every two or three years, and a further requirement that the court be kept clean and in order.

Mr. Prussin was persuaded by Miss Stringfellow and she carried the day. Mildred Jeanmaire Berendsen, who would become Chapin's fourth headmistress, gives her full credit for the negotiations. "The garage was going to be right next to the North Door. Miss Stringfellow persuaded them to put it on Eighty-fifth Street and to change the color of the bricks. She traded Chapin's light rights for those concessions. She was a very skillful woman."

The students watched 110 East End Avenue being built. Catherine Woodbridge, a teacher who later became headmistress of the Nightingale-Bamford School, remembers stopping her class in room 4D on the north side of the building and having everyone "lining up at the window when the concrete floor slab was poured just outside to our level. It was very fascinating to see how all the plumbing and electrical lines were laid out first and then the concrete poured over them like an enormous mud pie."

Miss Stringfellow appeared easygoing because of her laugh and her good nature, but she was also a stickler for etiquette and order. She made it clear, for example, that lunch and tea should be served formally, and she did not allow talking in the elevators or in the halls. Corinne Olli, who taught English during the 1940s and 1950s, told the story of a naval officer of high rank who came to Chapin as the Commencement speaker. "E.G.S. had assured him the exercises would begin at 11:00 A.M. and end promptly at noon, and of course they did. Already impressed by that fact, he watched with amazement as the girls filed out of the Assembly Room, carrying their folding chairs with them. Spontaneously the gentleman turned to E.G.S. and said, 'Good Heavens, Miss Stringfellow, you ought to be in the Navy!' "

When Linda Borock, who later became head of the physical education department, first met Miss Stringfellow, she had this impression: "I thought she was a caricature of some English person I had met in a novel. She was at once a lady, and at the same time so hearty and outspoken and direct. She seemed to do everything as if she was born to it." Mrs. Borock described her first visit to Chapin as a basketball referee in 1957:

I was met by the coaches and introduced to the two captains and we shook hands and the game began. I probably shouldn't have been paid for it because the students did most of the refereeing themselves. They indicated when they hit balls out of bounds, they

Mrs. Borock

Basketball circa 1953

raised their hands if they had committed a foul. All I could do was blow the whistle and have the scorers record it.

After the game was over, we were asked to stay for tea, an event I was certainly not anticipating.... We could see the large table covered with white linen or lace. There was a silver tea service at either end. Miss Stringfellow was pouring at one end, and the president of the Athletic Association at the other. There was another woman, dressed like the person at the front door, serving little tea sandwiches on a silver platter. There was a great deal of socialization and polite chatter. I remember thinking I hope I dropped bread crumbs on my way in, because I was certain I would not be able to find my way out.

Miss Stringfellow was generous to her staff and faculty outside as well as in the school. She gave away tickets to concerts and opera because she wanted people to be happy. When Miss Jennings's mother came to live with her daughter Frances, Miss Stringfellow bought a windowful of orchids to greet her. Mrs. Olli wrote of her years at Chapin, "I found every visit to

Miss Stringfellow's office a rewarding one. We would deal with whatever matter brought me there, and then, more often than not, E.G.S. would reminisce, her talk punctuated by my laughter. There was not much that she did not know about human nature. Nothing surprised her, and although her own standards of behavior were high, she had a humorous tolerance for the peccadilloes and inconsistencies of the human race."

Miss Whiteside

Mary Norman Whiteside arrived in 1944 to teach English and Latin, and stayed until 1980, becoming an integral part of the school both as an administrator—she became head of the Upper School—and teacher. She lost neither her southern accent nor her southern gentility over the years, and was never heard to utter an unkind word about anyone. Miss Whiteside was reputed to have said that if one of the teachers were absent, she would be happy to substitute because she could teach any subject except physical education. In retirement she qualified this statement, saying she could not teach either advanced mathematics or Greek. Alumnae remember her as kind, perceptive and tolerant. One alumna wrote of her, "When I visited Dove Cottage, Wordsworth's home, all the knowledge and insight that she had imparted flooded over me. Her patient way with a quiet student and her eagerness to communicate all that she had to share were among her strongest qualities."

Alumnae and faculty have commented on the rigors of a Chapin education during the 1940s and 1950s, and the work involved in getting into a prestigious college. Sandi Dinkins Britton '54 wrote,

Then as now, all of the city's top girls' schools were dedicated to qualifying their students for admission to the best colleges. At Chapin we were in school from 8:30 A.M. to 4:15 P.M. every day except Friday, and in the Upper School we coped with four to five hours of homework each night. Those of us who were serious about our studies were accepted not only by our first-choice colleges, but by every college we applied to. School assured us that honing our minds and learning to think for ourselves were essential to us as individuals. But because of the times we lived in, the messages we received from school, on the one hand, and from our families and society, on the other, were contradictory. Outside school, we learned that our education was meant to make us worthy companions to our husbands-to-be and better mothers to our future children. There wasn't much doubt about which message to believe.

Later, in 1966, the year she retired, Miss Lloyd-Thomas said, "If you don't go on to some further form of education nowadays you are made to feel like a dropout from civilized society. This is a revolution . . . the campus has supplanted the ballroom as the main matrimonial hunting ground."

The Cold War had increased the anxieties of the outside world, and within the school steps were taken to ensure order and security. The New York Housing Department inspector agreed it would be better to keep children in the building in case of an air raid, and to assemble them in the basement and the inside corridors of the first two floors. "We wore our tin dog tags and marched silently to the basement during the bomb drills." In 1953 faculty members were required to sign the following oath of allegiance administered by Miss Stringfellow:

> I do solemnly swear (or affirm) that I will support the constitution of the United States of America and the constitution of the State of New York, and I will faithfully discharge, according to the best of my ability, the duties of the position of........................ in The Chapin School, 100 East End Avenue, New York City, New York.

The year 1955 was a momentous one for the trustees. In January, Miss Stringfellow gave formal notice that she would like to retire at the end of the 1955–1956 school year, an action which did not, in fact, occur until June 1959. The trustees thought that "in a school whose traditions are so important an element there would be great advantages if a qualified candidate for the position can be found among the present faculty." Outside candidates were also to be considered. A search committee was duly appointed and went through all the necessary procedures, receiving suggestions, examining credentials and interviewing applicants.

In November 1955, the treasurer of the Board, Richard S. Perkins, brought up the matter of a campaign for increased endowment funds. The income would be used for teachers' salaries. In March of 1956, the Endowment Fund was renamed the Guaranty Fund, with a goal of $1,000,000. When completed, the sum of $1,375,000 was the largest amount ever raised by a girls' day school. It was at this time that Annual Giving was established.

Miss Stringfellow receiving her honorary degree from NYU in 1959

There was no diminution in Miss Stringfellow's powers toward the end of her career as headmistress. Her mind was as astute as ever, and her laugh still rang heartily through the halls. She had worked hard to open new worlds to the girls of the Chapin School both inside and outside the classroom. She had enriched and developed the curriculum, and she had maintained and attracted a highly qualified faculty. In addition, she had opened the doors of the school even wider to the alumnae and the parents. Most important, she had done it all without losing close touch with the children.

In 1959 New York University awarded Miss Stringfellow an honorary doctor of humane letters degree, and in 1960 Smith College did the same. Smith's citation read in part:

For fifty years you taught up and down all the grades of the Chapin School in New York City; for the last 24 of them you were its headmistress. Through this half-century, while revolutionary changes in the life, work and education of women were straining the adaptive powers of all schools and their teachers, you displayed the explorer's instinct for new possibilities, the traditionalist's concern for maintaining high standards, and your own deep sensitivity towards the problems of coming of age in a great city.

The NYU citation ended, "Well may she long embrace in retrospect the gratitude which finds poetic expression in the lines: 'I have taught them the goodness of knowledge/They have taught me the goodness of God.'"

There were innumerable efforts to immortalize Miss Stringfellow as she retired, but she was steadfast in her determination not to make speeches and not to have her contribution to the school written up in any publication. Furthermore, she did not wish to have her portrait painted. Eventually a compromise was reached, and funds raised by alumnae for her portrait were used to build the Ethel Grey Stringfellow Art Case in the front hall of the school, and for a lecture series in her name.

Miss Stringfellow did not slip away into obscurity. After a trip to Europe, she went on with her life with her customary gusto, enjoyed the opera and ran the Sunday School of St. James' Church, building it up through the sheer force of her personality. Possibly her one educational failure was her white Sealyham terrier, Winkie. Reportedly, "He ate turkey and lobster and such things and yapped all the time," and, "he bit quite a number of people, including his owner!"

Mrs. Berendsen paid tribute to her dear friend and mentor when she recalled Miss Stringfellow's section in Class Five arithmetic. "She came across the threshhold, as I was collecting my possessions; she would throw out to the Fives gathered there something like, 'Take 4, double it, double it again, triple it and add 2—what do you have?' 50. 50 years of inspired and joyous teaching in classrooms on 57th Street and in this building [100 East End Avenue]. If you add infinite quantities of courage, joy and generosity and humor—ADD to the nth power perception, vigor and faith in God, and undivided attention to encouraging the best that was in a student…we have only a token of the measurement of this remarkable woman." At Miss Stringfellow's last Board meeting, the Reverend Dr. Arthur L. Kinsolving, rector of St. James' Church, spoke for the trustees when he said, "It is not only that there is, in our opinion, no woman in this whole city who stands out as a finer citizen, and not only that the school she has guided and developed these many years enjoys currently a reputation second to none as a great educational institution, but that it is reassuring, in an era when one is so uncertain as to how far values have been clouded and confused, to find the whole community with virtual unanimity joining in admiration for this truly great, creative, Christian educator."

An intimation of the great affection the students and parents of Chapin felt for Miss Stringfellow is a song written by Lois Blagden (Mrs. Edward S. Blagden), the mother of Emma Blagden '37, during her daughter's final year at the school. Set to the tune of "Funiculi, Funicula," it was always sung with great spirit by the students.

Come let us sing a song enthusiastic
To one we know, to one we know
Who rules us all with measures firm and drastic,
Miss Stringfellow, Miss Stringfellow.
Her frown can make a sinner most terrific
Shake in her shoes, shake in her shoes.
Her smile is guaranteed the best specific
To cure the blues, to cure the blues.
Sing then, sing then to Miss Stringfellow
Bring then, bring then every art you know
To make it clear that she's a dear
And we are here to tell her so
Hail Miss Stringfellow!
Our love for you will ever grow!

CHAPTER FIVE

THE WHEEL TURNS

Counselor to the World.

HARRY HAVEMEYER, PRESIDENT,
BOARD OF TRUSTEES, 1969–1980,
ON MRS. BERENDSEN

There is little doubt that Miss Stringfellow's most successful experiment in hiring teachers directly from college was Mildred Jeanmaire Berendsen. Miss Jeanmaire came to Chapin in 1949 from Smith College, where she had been an honors history major. The first official mention of the young teacher appeared in the March 14, 1949, Board minutes: "Miss Mildred Jeanmaire…will take over Miss Wilkinson's ancient, medieval and modern history courses in Classes Eight, Nine and Ten, and also the History of Art course offered to Classes Eleven or Twelve. Miss Stringfellow expresses her special pleasure in this appointment, as it will show the school's support of the drive now being carried on in some of the major colleges to interest able young women in the teaching profession, and will give Miss Jeanmaire an opportunity to develop her courses and her classroom technique under Miss Wilkinson's guidance."

Where did this slim, twenty-one-year-old girl find the courage to undertake such a formidable teaching assignment? The vast scope of knowledge necessary to teach so many different courses was daunting in itself, but to succeed Miss Wilkinson, and to teach under her watchful

Mrs. Berendsen

Julia Benik

Annie Drobney

Ann Rose Bodisch

and critical eye, was a gargantuan challenge. Was it the innocence of youth, the confidence of total ignorance or some inner steel and fire? Later Mrs. Berendsen recalled her first visit to the Chapin School:

> I arrived at Chapin for an interview when I was a senior at Smith. I couldn't find the school because there was no name on the building but thought, "oh, maybe this is it" and began wrestling with the doorknob of 100 East End Avenue. It didn't turn. Finally I rang the bell. It got worse when Julia [who greeted visitors] answered the door in her black uniform and white apron. "Oh my goodness," said I. "I've come to an embassy!" "No," she said, "you are at The Chapin School."
>
> I waited in a rather dreary room to the left of the front door. Shortly a woman came through the door, and I stood up and said, "Miss Stringfellow," and she said, "no, I'm Lucy Powell, Miss Stringfellow's secretary."
>
> At this point as a person coming to an interview, I was not feeling very confident. I went into Miss Stringfellow's office, and Miss Stringfellow couldn't have been more cordial with her very strong southern accent, which took me aback given that this was a New York school, and we had a very pleasant conversation. She was very welcoming and made me feel very comfortable.

Two of the future Mrs. Berendsen's character traits emerge from this story: her confidence in her abilities and her total lack of pretension or conceit. Her parents had emigrated from Switzerland shortly before she was born and she had grown up in Brooklyn. Education was highly valued by her community of first-generation Americans and she had always worked hard in school. She was an exceptionally good student and had been girl leader of Arista, the honors society at James Madison High School, where, she recalls, "the boys got most of the attention. Although I took science every year, I never had a female teacher and never did an experiment."

Several weeks after her interview, Mildred Jeanmaire came home from Smith to attend a friend's wedding. She was busy doing her laundry when the phone rang. It was Miss Powell calling for Miss Stringfellow to offer her a teaching position at the Chapin School for the following year.

From the beginning, Miss Jeanmaire put her heart and soul into her job:

> I lived in the back of Miss Whiteside's room, but I assisted Mlle. Duloux, the Class Eight homeroom teacher, with the blue slips on which the teachers wrote the assignments if you were absent. They had to be circulated and picked up, and I ended up having to do that. By the time I got upstairs to the lunchroom on the fifth floor, occasionally I had to eat with Miss Stringfellow because all the other places were taken. I was so nervous I don't know how I ate. In addition, I never taught in the same room twice. I carried huge cumbersome maps everywhere. I lugged boxes of slides. I lost weight. My mother was ready to call Miss Stringfellow to find out what they were doing to me. I was teaching five courses: two Eights, a Nine, a Ten and History of Art.

She was also the chaperone on the school bus, commuting from Brooklyn by subway each morning to Forty-eighth Street, where she boarded the vehicle. Nicky Stout Chapin '52, a student when Mrs. Berendsen first came to the school and later a member of the faculty for forty-three years, remembers that she and her friends were in agreement that such a young, pretty lady could not be a teacher and must be a student in disguise.

One of Mrs. Berendsen's early students, who later became a trustee, remembers her history class: "She was coming! The staccato tap of her high heels echoed in the quiet hall. Arms laden, she burst through the door and the class began. The pace was fast and electrifying. The chalk clattered across the board as people and places came alive. Her expectations were high and we strove to please her. There was no doubt that she was an authority figure and we couldn't have grasped the scant number of years that separated us in age from our teacher."

Mildred Jeanmaire married Charles G. Berendsen, an engineering student, the summer after her first year at Chapin. Back at the school in the fall, the new Mrs. Berendsen was gaining experience. She discovered that "Chapin students and their families have unusual resources." One day when she was reviewing the Russian Revolution with one of her history classes, a student revealed that Aleksandr Kerensky, the head of the provisional Russian government of 1917 that had been overthrown in the Bolshevik Revolution, was living at her house. Mrs. Berendsen invited Mr. Kerensky to speak at News, which he did "in this most enormous voice that could have been heard in Chicago."

Several years after Mrs. Berendsen arrived, Miss Stringfellow wrote, "More schools are interested in taking girls right out of college as teachers because of their success here. Their success, too, has pointed up the fact that a full liberal arts course is the best basis for teaching any subject, and that native ability is of more value than courses in educational technique."

In 1956 Mrs. Berendsen was offered the position of assistant to the headmistress, duties to begin in September of that year. As assistant to Miss Stringfellow, Mrs. Berendsen was admitted to membership in the Head Mistresses Association of the East and the National Association of Principals of Schools for Girls. She also represented Miss Stringfellow at the Guild for Independent Schools. Concerning Mrs. Berendsen, it was later reported that "the comments that came to Miss Stringfellow from the Heads of other schools had been without exception favorable. Within the Chapin School group she has been fully accepted by the teachers and the girls. The Fine Arts Club, of which she was asked to be faculty advisor, has grown from its beginnings last year with eight members to a membership this year of 32." Mrs. Berendsen served as assistant hostess at Club parties and at tea for teams after interschool games. Whatever she was asked to do, she did it well.

Mrs. Berendsen was appointed assistant headmistress for the year 1957–1958. The Board asked Miss Stringfellow to notify Mrs. Berendsen that it was the expectation that she would be named associate headmistress for the year 1958–1959 and, upon Miss Stringfellow's retirement in June 1959, unless something unforeseen occurred, she would be named headmistress of the school. She had been invited to attend meetings of the Board at Miss Stringfellow's request for over a year. "After full discussion, the Trustees present expressed their unanimous approval of Mrs. Berendsen's designation as Miss Stringfellow's successor." In 1958 the Berendsens moved to 80 East End Avenue and the headmistress-to-be stopped riding the school bus.

At the Alumnae Luncheon in April 1959, approximately 350 alumnae came, as a report in the 1959 *Alumnae Bulletin* noted, "to pay homage to Miss Stringfellow on the 50th anniversary of her arrival at the Chapin School, and to greet our new Headmistress, Mrs. Berendsen." Miss Stringfellow wrote as she retired, "It is with complete confidence that I turn over the School to her, knowing that it will go on to greater heights under her inspiring leadership."

The world Miss Stringfellow had inhabited so comfortably had been transformed. After World War II and the anxieties of the Cold War came McCarthyism and the Korean War. The hydrogen bomb was tested in 1952. In 1953, scientists mapped the structure of DNA, and in 1957 *Sputnik,* followed in 1958 by *Explorer* 1, marked the beginning of the Space Age. The Computer Age was beginning. Nuclear power was generated on a viable industrial scale by 1956 in Britain. Scientists were beginning to worry about our environment and sponsored the first International Geophysical Year in 1957.

Mrs. Berendsen in 1959

When a new head is installed at a school, changes are to be expected. Under Mildred Berendsen's administration, the changes were constant, and, in large part, they were dictated by the times. Societal changes were dramatic. The Civil Rights movement was gaining momentum. Public schools in Little Rock, Arkansas, were desegregated in 1955, and black writers like Ralph Ellison and James Baldwin became prominent figures. Theatergoers were flocking to the avant-garde plays of Samuel Beckett, Eugène Ionesco and Jean Genet, while English playwrights like John Osborne and Harold Pinter galvanized American audiences with their portrayals of British disillusionment with contemporary life. Rock-and-roll music was born, and Elvis Presley became its most popular vocalist. Modern sound and video techniques were invented. Kinetic, Pop and Op Art emerged. The death of parental peace occurred in 1959 when stereophonic records came on the market. Youth was on the march, and the young in America, just prior to the Vietnam War, were influenced by the works of the Beat Generation—Jack Kerouac,

William S. Burroughs, Henry Miller, Allen Ginsberg—who sought "spontaneous living" and the means to express it. Their drug-suffused, iconoclastic lifestyle had tremendous allure. The sexual revolution gained converts with the advent of oral contraceptives in 1960.

Under Mrs. Berendsen's guidance, life at Chapin was orderly and goal-oriented. Chapin students gained the confidence to tackle their own careers and professions. Mrs. Berendsen worked hard and respected the traditions of the school, and did not move at once to change the uniform or the formal atmosphere, the teas and the unspoken rules of conduct in the lunchroom and in the halls. "She was a perfectionist and paid great attention to details." One of the earliest and most noticeable changes to the building in her administration, one that had been initiated by Miss

Playing on the roof, circa 1954

Middle School lunch in the fifth-floor dining room, circa 1967

Stringfellow, was the enclosure of the roof to create an all-weather gymnasium. Trustee Margaret Henderson Bailie oversaw the design of the room. Her contributions to the school as a landscape architect, designer and wise and generous friend were far-reaching. Some of Miss Chapin's possessions came to the school from Mrs. Bailie, who grew up adoring her combination headmistress and godmother. When she died in 1976, the Board remembered her as "a searcher for truth who always insisted on the best for the school founded by her great friend, Maria Bowen Chapin."

A small but significant change was the designation of a room on the fifth floor for a faculty smoking lounge. Mrs. Berendsen recalled, "The last year Miss Stringfellow was there I spoke to her about her policy of making teachers smoke outside the building. 'Mildred, when you are head of School, you may let them smoke in the school, but while I am head, they may not.'" (By 1993 teachers were smoking outside again and the school became smoke-free as concern about the health hazards of smoking intensified.)

In 1961 a Curriculum Committee was set up to reevaluate the course of study in the Upper School. There had already been some changes. Geography was expanded to cover all parts of the world. The two-year course in American history for Elevens and Twelves was dropped in favor of a one-year course in American history followed by a course in twentieth-century history. More hours were allotted to English, mathematics and history in the Middle and Upper Schools. Advanced-placement courses, which had been initiated across the country in the late 1950s, were now offered in all major subjects.

Science in the Lower and Middle Schools had always been a popular and well-taught subject. Biology included botany, with work in the greenhouse, and human physiology. Girls began thinking of careers in science, and their growing concern for the environment encouraged the school to schedule more field trips and lab courses. Biology was introduced in Class Eight, physical science in Nine, chemistry in Ten, advanced-placement physics in Eleven and advanced-placement biology in Twelve. An elective in astronomy was offered.

Mrs. Ruth Hutter, who became head of the Upper School mathematics department in 1967, revitalized the math curriculum. Chapin allowed her the freedom to use her own methods rather than follow the popular trends. She introduced calculus and helped students overcome their fear of mathematics. She felt that math anxiety need not exist, that every student could succeed and that girls were definitely not mathematically inferior to boys.

From its earliest days, the school had been searching for a legible, distinctive style of handwriting. However, the round block roman lettering of Chapin penmanship made the children slow writers, and in the 1950s there was a clamor for a speedier, cursive hand. The Class One room teacher, Miss Janes, was convinced of the superiority of italic script, and in 1960 italic writing was introduced in Classes Four and Five on a trial basis. In 1962, Paul Standard, a teacher of calligraphy at Cooper Union and the Parsons School of Design, gave a lecture demonstration to the entire faculty and, through the year, gave lessons to Lower and Middle School teachers. Thus, italic script became the official handwriting of the school. Ultimately, italic handwriting proved unpopular with the faculty at large. It was discontinued around 1970 in favor of the Palmer method and then a similar program.

Diversifying the student body had been under discussion as early as 1944, when Miss Stringfellow had been hostess for an all-day meeting on Race Tolerance. Mrs. Berendsen now led discussions on admitting students of color to the school. By 1964 she was able to report that the first African-American student had been taken into Class Six. At a meeting of the Board in June 1967, she reported that the school had been in touch with several families interested in an independent school education through the East Harlem Protestant Parish. "We have accepted a girl in Class One, and hope to admit others." In November 1967 Mrs. Berendsen was happy to say that children who had come to Chapin through the East Harlem Protestant Parish were succeeding at the school. By September 1970 there were seventeen students of color in the school. A new black studies club, Pepukayi, meaning "wake up" was established in 1971, the year that Chapin's first African-American student, Jacqueline Holland Higgins, graduated. The number of students of color continued to increase, and the leadership of the school as affirmed by the young women at Chapin included six students of color as presidents of Self-Government between 1983 and 2000. Marlen Bodden '79, who came to the school from Honduras in 1975, was to become Chapin's first alumna trustee of color in 1995.

For many students of color the emotional adjustment was painful. Wanda Holland '85, who came to Chapin in 1981, explained, "Students come here feeling like aliens. They look around and see people who come from a different world, who speak a different language, who go off to Morocco or Hong Kong or to the Caribbean on Christmas vacation. These classmates have access to privileges and experiences totally outside a minority student's reach."

Wanda added that confidence in oneself and pride in being African American were the keys to a successful adjustment. "That's what distinguishes children of color who come to Chapin and have a good time here and those who really feel wounded by the experience." Wanda went on to be a member of Chapin's faculty from 1990 to 1997.

Another African-American student wrote, "Maybe some of you still don't have an idea of what I'm about. If not, I'll sum it up like this: when I go to school every day I wonder why everyone can't live the way people on 86th Street do, with doormen, clean lobbies and well-paying jobs. I guess it's just the way life is. What I'm going to do is to try to change that any way I can, so that the children of those who grew up with me will see a better life than their parents or grandparents did."

Mrs. Berendsen was, in the words of one of her students, "always a strong advocate for students of color and she did all that was possible to help them come to Chapin and other independent schools in New York City." She was elected to the boards of two educational programs,

Miss Phelps

Mr. Walker

Miss Neale

A Better Chance and Early Steps. A Better Chance (ABC) looks for gifted public school children who would benefit from a private high school education; Early Steps is a feeder for kindergarten and elementary schools. Lance Odden, headmaster of the Taft School, recently wrote, "In the 1980s, when the ABC talent search program encountered tough financial sledding as money for minority education contracted, it fell to a number of school heads to save ABC, and no one rose more powerfully to the challenge than did Millie Berendsen. She hosted endless meetings.... She measured every program in terms of what it offered children and schools. ABC survived because of her firm and loving leadership." Chapin also joined a third program for minority youth called Prep for Prep, which was established in 1978. Diversity, so imperative for the strength of the school as it approached the twenty-first century, had become an issue that would grow in importance.

Although the Chapin curriculum was sound, it was solidly Western in orientation. To expand its parameters, Mrs. Berendsen introduced a number of non-Western electives in the Upper School, including courses in Indian, African, Chinese and Japanese history.

Judith Phelps, a graduate of Middlebury College with a master's degree from Columbia University, arrived at Chapin in 1961, along with Louise Henderson and Charles Walker. After proving her mettle teaching the Eights, Nines and Tens, Miss Phelps helped reorganize the Upper School English curriculum.

Miss Henderson, a graduate of Wellesley College with a master's degree from Stanford University, taught ancient, medieval, European and American history her first year at Chapin, and became an institution. Her irrepressible brio, good sense and administrative abilities qualified her to be not only an assistant to the headmistress but eventually the Class Eight room teacher, and Chapin's legendary college guidance counselor.

Aided by Robert Schrade, Mr. Walker continued to strengthen Chapin's music department. He had been an organist and choirmaster in Paris and at the Church of the Heavenly Rest in New York. His love of music strongly influenced the students. Under Mr. Walker's direction, the Choral Club performed at Avery Fisher Hall with the Canterbury Choral Society, which he had founded. Lower School girls bonged away on the Orff instruments—glockenspiels, xylophones, bells, wood blocks and triangles—and then went on to study the recorder in Class Three.

Vivian Neale, who succeeded Miss Lloyd-Thomas as head of the classics department, strengthened the classical tradition by introducing Latin in Class Seven, offering two advanced-placement courses in Latin in the Upper School, and keeping Greek in the curriculum.

Report books were revised. Each subject teacher was to give a grade not only for achievement but also a number to indicate the student's effort and attitude in that subject. Lower and Middle School students were required to put in longer days to strengthen their preparation for the demands of the Upper School.

Mrs. Berendsen allayed worries that so many changes would alter the spirit of the school. "The framework of Self-Government and the academic program are not so firmly outlined that there is no room for individual change or adaptation, but it exists as a guideline which the past found suitable and worthy to be passed on. This is the quality we must retain! It is in this spirit that the School continues. We are always aware of the remarkable heritage of accomplishment which is ours, but we are ever searching for the ways and means to serve the present community of students."

One service to the community was the revision of Self-Government. From 1963 on, Self-Government became, as an alumna put it, "less of a student organization that looked inward and meted out punishment for transgressions and patrolled the halls and Dining Room, and more of an organization that looked outward in a spirit of community service." Girls guided visitors about the school, served as audiovisual technicians, worked as teacher aides in the Lower School, processed books in the library and responded in general to the needs of the school.

During Mrs. Berendsen's first decade as headmistress, cataclysmic changes occurred in America and in the world. The feminist movement encouraged women to reexamine their role in society. Even before the controversial Vietnam War, which tore the country apart, the United States had been traumatized by the building of the Berlin Wall in 1961, the Cuban missile crisis in 1962, and the assassination of President Kennedy in 1963. While the United States, the U.S.S.R. and Britain signed a nuclear test ban treaty in 1963, China exploded its first nuclear bomb in 1964. The Civil Rights movement received a terrible blow when Martin Luther King Jr. was assassinated in 1968. Although he left a legacy of peaceful protest, many African Americans, influenced by Eldridge Cleaver and Malcolm X, now advocated violent protest. The counterculture that had blossomed in the United States, partly in sympathy with the Beat Generation and partly in response to the Vietnam War, advocated communes and anarchism. "Make love, not war" had become a national slogan. The songs that young people listened to became increasingly cynical and sexually provocative. Family life was under pressure. The divorce rate escalated. Many women went back to school or joined the workforce.

It was not an easy time to head a school. As Miss Whiteside wrote, "The late 1960s was a time when there was more likely to be rebellion against anything that was standard, rebellion no matter what was being taught and the way it was taught. The students had a different approach to life. Often their issues were: 'why should we read something that was written so far back? Why can't we read things that are contemporary?'" She found that many students no longer sympathized with Tess of the d'Urbervilles, a woman trapped by circumstance, although a few still wept at her plight.

Students were interested in and concerned about issues of social justice they had never considered before. They not only wanted to know how much money was being spent on scholarships, but also wanted to raise money for them. They anguished over the people starving in Biafra. They embraced the goals of the Civil Rights movement and wanted to be part of it. They were opposed to the Vietnam War and sympathetic to the antiwar demonstrations on college campuses. In response to these issues, the Peace and Freedom Club and the Truth Club, whose membership was limited to girls in Classes Ten, Eleven and Twelve, were formed in 1968.

The girls wanted to have more contact with the faculty. To satisfy this desire, the school organized informal discussion periods or coffee hours in the faculty room and formed a student-faculty Honor Code Committee to talk over the standards by which the school lived.

When Robert Kennedy was assassinated, on the night before Commencement in 1968, one senior felt "a stunning sense of loss, which dominated that morning as much as the moment of graduation itself, and seemed to emphasize the effect of a dividing line in personal experience." *Newsweek* editor Osborn Elliott, the Commencement speaker, said that adults should be grateful that the younger generation is not apathetic about the ills of our civilization. "I say keep heating it up—but let the heat be accompanied by some light. Don't settle for things as they are, but don't settle either for just tearing them down. Don't settle for the modish cliché of the moment. Probe, challenge, demand answers—and supply some answers of your own." Mrs. Berendsen and the girls were deeply moved by Mr. Elliott's speech, and Mrs. Berendsen was in tune with his thinking. "We, who are teachers, must be sure to continue to impress on the young respect for others' ideas, for research and truth, for integrity. We must convey to students that education is not a right but a privilege."

For students as well as their parents, the 1960s were both frightening and exciting. After the failed Bay of Pigs invasion and the Cuban missile crisis, some parents took their children out of school and sent them to New England. In this instance and in many others, Mrs. Berendsen talked to parents, students and faculty. As she listened, counseled and soothed, she became, in the words of Anne Finch Cox '36, "a one-woman community center." Harry Havemeyer, president of the Board of Trustees from 1969 to 1980, referred to her as "counselor to the world." Everyone came to her with their problems. One student said, "We were all her children." An alumna remembers Mrs. Berendsen's telling her in Class Eleven that she'd be unemployable for life if she didn't go to college. "She appealed to my ego by letting me apply early admission to Sarah Lawrence. I'll never forget her bursting into a class to tell me I'd gotten in."

Mrs. Berendsen never gave up on a girl who was in trouble, but she never let her shrink from the consequences of her actions. "I never expelled anyone. I believe in redemption. I gave them a chance to think twice about what they had done, and they had to live with it in an environment where people knew what they had done." One very rude ninth-grader was asked to come to her office. "I said 'you don't have to be a genius, but you must be respectful of the people in this building who are teaching you and who believe in the school's policy.' Three years later, Commencement morning, the girl asked to see me. She came to tell me the best day of her life was the day I hauled her into my office. 'You made me take charge of my life.' "

Anxiety increased as family life became less structured. Mothers were at work, nannies and governesses were figures from another era, and rules and regulations were vanishing fast. The school was one place students could look to for guidance, and Chapin tried to teach them what they must know to live in a world where they were less protected than in the past. Accordingly, teachers encouraged students to talk more in class and marked them on class participation. Girls were no longer counseled by Miss Stringfellow's dictum to be "conspicuous by being inconspicuous," but, as Mrs. Berendsen declared, to "stand up and be counted." As

Miss Stringfellow and Mrs. Berendsen at the groundbreaking ceremony for a new wing, June 1969

a good mother would do, Mrs. Berendsen also counseled her students "to sleep eight hours a night, not eight hours a week."

Throughout the 1960s Mrs. Berendsen had asked prominent speakers to come to Chapin. Richard Nixon gave the Commencement address in 1964, Louis Auchincloss in 1965 and William F. Buckley Jr. in 1969. Girls listened to lectures by John Ciardi, the poet; Vera Micheles Dean, the foreign policy authority; Theodore Sorenson, a speechwriter for President Kennedy; and Dr. Judianne Densen-Gerber, the head of Odyssey House, a drug rehabilitation center. Osborn Elliott moderated a panel of speakers on national affairs, international events and scientific achievements. Their range of topics reflected the turbulent times.

Last, but hardly least of the jobs Mrs. Berendsen tackled in the 1960s was the capital fund drive endorsed by the Board in June 1967. Known as the Chapin School Development Fund and chaired by trustees and parents Deirdre Spencer Adler '42 and William E. Jackson, its goal was to raise at least $2,500,000 for a building addition and faculty salaries.

For years the school had needed major alterations. Space was at a premium. In January 1967, the question of buying the building to the west of the school owned by the Dominican Sisters of the Sick Poor was seriously considered. Initial efforts to purchase it were not successful, and the decision was made that it was best to build a smaller building over a portion of the school's yard. In June 1969, a vigorous Miss Stringfellow dug her spade into the ground at Chapin's groundbreaking ceremony for the new wing that was to be built. Then, due in large part to the efforts of Board chairman Polly Rousmaniere Gordon '28, the Sisters reconsidered, and in November 1969 the convent was sold to Chapin for $600,000. Similar in style to the main school building, it had been designed by Delano & Aldrich and built in 1930. This building was to be called the Ethel Grey Stringfellow Wing. But the happy task of moving into the wing had hardly begun when the Chapin family had to pause, sadly, and say a final farewell to its third remarkable headmistress.

Miss Stringfellow celebrating her eightieth birthday at the 1967 Alumnae Luncheon

In February 1970 Miss Stringfellow suffered a heart attack, from which she recovered. When in May she had the stroke that would end her life, Mrs. Berendsen was called, and she arrived at once for a last visit. Miss Stringfellow had given instructions that she was not to be moved, and she died peacefully at home on May 8 shortly after the visit from her beloved protégée. The Reverend Ralph R. Warren Jr. conducted her funeral service at St. James' Church, which was crowded with former students and friends. The school was closed for the day so that the girls could attend, wearing the uniform Miss Stringfellow had chosen for them in the thirties, and which Mrs. Berendsen had not yet changed. The Madrigals, composed of Chapin's best choral voices, and the Twelves, who were in Class One when Miss Stringfellow retired, sang the benediction. Mrs. Berendsen remembers how glad she was to have waited to change the uniform. "When Miss Stringfellow was buried, she was surrounded by the girls in the uniform she loved." The obituary read that there were no survivors. "But in that jam-packed church were all the survivors." One alumna said the bells that rang at the end of the service reminded her of Miss Stringfellow's wonderful laugh.

At Prayers the day after the funeral, Mrs. Berendsen spoke of Miss Stringfellow. "Hers was a joyous spirit who gave of herself freely, whose strength derived from a strong faith in God, whose faith in us made us accomplish tasks we could not have done otherwise, whose love of people always established unique relationships." These same qualities were woven into the fiber of Mildred Berendsen's being; Miss Stringfellow would live on in her chosen successor.

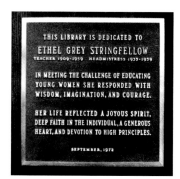

Dedication plaque for the
Ethel Grey Stringfellow Library

The Library 1928–1972, now the Berendsen Room

Before making any extensive renovations to the new wing, it was thought wise to "live" in it for a while. However, the creation of a multipurpose dining area and new kitchen on the site of the school's yard got the immediate go-ahead. By September 1970, Chapin's first computer had been installed in the wing and classes were being held there in mathematics, history of art and Lower School dance.

In January 1971, plans were finalized for remodeling the first floor of the wing for the music department and the second and third floors for use by the Lower School. The kitchen, boilers and multipurpose room were finally completed by June 1971.

The multipurpose room would be renamed the Mary Rousmaniere Gordon Room in 1980, in recognition of Polly Gordon's many contributions, particularly her crucial role in acquiring the Stringfellow wing. In 1985 her husband, Albert H. Gordon, established the Mary Rousmaniere Gordon Fellowship Fund in memory of Mrs. Gordon for summer study/travel to enhance the professional life of faculty members. Mrs. Berendsen described the fellowships as "a special opportunity for enrichment and renewal" and "a unique support for teachers whose talent and energy fuel the students' commitment to their studies."

In January 1972 work began on the Ethel Grey Stringfellow Library, located where the lunchroom had been on the fifth floor of the main building. Completed in September of the same year, it contained 25,000 volumes. The librarian, Nancy Bartlett, described in Chapin's fall newsletter how handsome the library was, owing to the sense of color, light and design of the chief architect, Mr. Herbert Shalat of the firm of Bloch, Hesse & Shalat. "Red carpet, blue chairs, and rich brown wood-work are cheerful with sun on good days and fluorescent light coves on cloudy ones. It is also an eminently practical library."

The crossover between the fourth floor of the main building and the new wing took longer to complete, as did the biology and science rooms on the fourth floor. Everyone concerned seemed to take the noise and rubble of the construction in their stride. Reflecting a Board decision to reincorporate a kindergarten into the Chapin program, plans for new classroom space were drawn up in May 1973. Miss Chapin had not thought it necessary to continue the Kindergarten when the school moved to East End Avenue because other opportunities for learning at that level were available. For some time Mrs. Berendsen had contemplated reinstituting a kindergarten in order to remain competitive with other girls' schools that had kindergartens. There were also plans for extensive renovations in the basement providing for expansion of the nurse's office, improved house staff quarters, a student lounge and the remodeling of the basement corridor known as the Holland Tunnel.

Finally the renovation, with its many phases, was complete. In her fall 1974 report, the headmistress praised Mr. Shalat's work. He had, she

The Junior Council, circa 1971

Mrs. Berendsen conducting Prayers

said, "articulated the needs of the Chapin School of the present while remaining sensitive to the intrinsic beauty of the building."

With the student uprisings at Columbia University and the violence in Chicago during the Democratic Convention in the wake of the assassinations of Martin Luther King Jr. and Robert Kennedy, 1968 and 1969 had been particularly difficult years. On May 4, 1970, Ohio National Guardsmen fired into a crowd of student demonstrators at Kent State University, a normally peaceful campus. The fusillade killed four students and wounded eleven others. For the rest of the school year seventy-five campuses remained closed while student protests flared in the surrounding communities.

Mrs. Berendsen held firm. Chapin remained open. Discussions reflecting students' feelings led to changes within the school. The entire

The new yard

school no longer congregated for Prayers at the beginning of each day, but only on Friday mornings. The Upper School met separately on Mondays and Wednesdays and the Lower and Middle Schools on Tuesdays and Thursdays. As Prayers became more pertinent to each age level, and the faculty became more involved, it became less of a religious exercise and more of a communal time to make announcements and discuss important issues.

The physical education department was revised and expanded under the direction of Mrs. Borock. She explained that traditionally a gym class had been a place to "go have a good time, release your energies, throw the ball around. Now gym teachers know more about how children grow—academically, psychologically and physically." In the 1970s gym classes were taught progressively over the grade levels, similar to a curriculum that builds on what students had learned in previous years. From Kindergarten on, a systematic approach to fitness ensured a certain level of competence. "It is important for a girl's self-confidence that she feel she has athletic ability. We're living in a time when you must be assertive in order to do what you want to do in life. Years ago we were told not to be too assertive, because assertive and aggressive moved together. Now being assertive is a very good thing."

Chapin's curriculum was under constant review. Electives in the Upper School were expanded every year. Beginning Spanish was offered in Classes Ten and Eleven. Advanced-placement math was offered in Class Twelve in addition to four elective courses in English and art history. The science program continued to grow. Earth science became part of the Middle School curriculum. Increased demand for science courses that related to nuclear energy and the Space Age led to a trimester requirement in nuclear energy for Class Eight in 1973–1974.

In the middle 1970s faculty members began participating in classes outside their discipline. An art teacher might explain aesthetics in a philosophy class or a science teacher discuss Einstein's theory of relativity in European history. In 1976, Class Eight engaged in a week-long humanities unit on eighteenth-century European history, presented by teachers from all disciplines, sometimes assisted by Class Twelve students studying at an advanced-placement level. One Class Eight study elaborately interwove English and French art with music and dance in the eighteenth century. A music course was available to Classes Ten, Eleven and Twelve to prepare girls for specific concerts, ballet programs, chamber music and opera. Elective art courses were expanded.

During this period, Chapin placed a greater emphasis on parent-school relations. Many parents wanted to be more involved in what was going on in the school, and Mrs. Berendsen eagerly encouraged them. In the late 1960s a draft of bylaws by Charlotte Binger Hasen '41 for a Chapin School Parents' Association was approved by the Board. The Association consisted of four parent officers: chairman, vice-chairman, treasurer, and secretary, and two parent representatives from each class. The chairman of the Association was to serve as an ex-officio member of the Board of Trustees. Elizabeth Mason Walbridge '35, who became the first chairman, conducted the initial meeting of the Parents' Association on October 22, 1969. Within four years the Parents' Association was providing a gymnastics program for fifty children as well as needlework classes, a film series and swimming, tennis and skating programs. In 1973 the association organized the school's first book fair, and in 1975, a neighborhood safety patrol.

The Parents' Association formed an Arts Committee that offered tickets to various Broadway and off-Broadway performances, the New York City Ballet's production of *The Nutcracker* and the New York Philharmonic's Young Philharmonic Series. Parents worked as volunteers in the school's library and in after-school programs for the students, and got involved in community activities such as the Eighty-fourth Street Block Association Fair. They even offered their babies as "demonstration models" for the Class Six course in baby care. Orientation meetings for new parents were inaugurated.

One of the most popular innovations in the school was the introduction of the new uniform in 1971. Upper School girls now sported dress Gordon plaid kilts with blouses and sweaters in colors that coordinated with the kilt. A white blouse was required for official occasions. Conflict over the blouses, which had to have a collar, led to turtlenecks as an alternative. Knee socks and shoes of the latest fashion were originally worn with the kilt, giving way in the eighties to sneakers. The familiar green bloomers and a white Chapin shirt served as the gym uniform. Several years later, the younger girls traded in their aqua linen tunics for drip-dry ones of yellow or green cord, and by 1977 bloomers had been exchanged for shorts.

Mrs. Berendsen wanted the school to be more involved in the city, to give the girls an opportunity to visit with students from other schools, to attend some coeducational classes. Interschool, a six-school organization composed of Brearley, Browning, Chapin, Collegiate, Nightingale-Bamford and Spence, and which later expanded to include Dalton and Trinity, was established in September of 1971 to provide opportunities that would otherwise not be available to the individual schools. It made academic courses such as Chinese history and Russian available when one school alone could not sustain such an offering. In 1974 apprenticeships were offered through Interschool to students by Mount Sinai Hospital, *Ms.* magazine, the American Museum of Natural History, the ASPCA, the Lenox Hill Neighborhood Association and Planned Parenthood. A major event evolving from Interschool was a College Night at which eleventh-grade students from the participating schools and their parents met with college representatives and college guidance counselors. However, scheduling presented problems, and by the 1990s Interschool had evolved into an administrative body that fostered communication between the schools and helped set policies.

Getting into college was now a procedure that involved much effort by the school, the students and the parents. When Miss Stringfellow was headmistress, she suggested which colleges would be best for each student, then had Miss Powell, her secretary, write the letters of recom-

Miss Henderson

Mrs. Mestrovic

mendation. When Mrs. Berendsen began her tenure, she handled the increasingly complex job of college guidance and, aided by personal and informal faculty comments, wrote all the college recommendations herself. However, in 1971 Miss Henderson returned to Chapin after a period as headmistress of the Sunset Hill School in Kansas City, Missouri, where she also had been a college guidance counselor. She thus seemed the ideal person to take over the time-consuming job. Miss Henderson tackled her new assignment with confidence and high spirits. She clearly thrived in her role. Teaching history to Class Eight established a relationship with the students and provided her with perspective on the girls' academic and personal growth.

Jane Mestrovic, who came to Chapin in 1963 with a master's degree in mathematics from Hunter College, brought Chapin into the technological age. Chapin's first computer took the form of a modern typewriter keyboard connected to a mainframe computer by telephone lines. As technology advanced, Mrs. Mestrovic led the school forward. When the school bought its first Apple computer, she introduced computer classes to both the Lower and Middle Schools, teaching the teachers along with their students. *The Chapin Chip,* a computer magazine by Middle School girls, was first issued in 1982, and by 1984 Chapin boasted eighteen Apples. Computer science became a separate department in 1985.

Mrs. Berendsen with the members of the Class of 1971 who entered the school as she became headmistress

Expansion into the new Ethel Grey Stringfellow Wing had proved to be a blessing. Lower School students enjoyed their new space. Nineteen Kindergarten students arrived in 1974 and settled into the wonderful new room, which contained a small kitchen and had its own bathroom. Space for outdoor play lay adjacent to it. By 1978 the Kindergarten had increased to forty-six students in two rooms. Class One students had homerooms and desks of their own. Twos and Threes were happy in small rooms, which allowed for a freer teaching situation and a less competitive atmosphere. A well-equipped new science room was on the third floor of the building. The choral room on the first floor was arranged like a small theater and equipped with permanent audiovisual machines. The Lower School library had windows on three sides and carpeting on the floor. Lunch hour became distinctly less formal in the new multipurpose room, which held 440 people and could be divided into three rooms.

Feminism, always an integral thread in the life of the school, became more marked in the seventies. Career Day, initiated in 1974, was termed a "projection into the future for the Upper School by interested alumnae, parents and friends." Girls were taken to various places in the city that might light a career path. "It was not our intention to 'brainwash' the girls into careers, but rather to make them aware of the specific kind of requirements needed for some careers and the tremendous variety of education which could pertain in other careers." In 1976 students visited the Legal Aid Society, the offices of the *New York Times, Glamour* magazine and a rehearsal of a Broadway play. They observed an operation at Mount Sinai Hospital and saw autistic patients at Bellevue. "The message was very strong that we were expected to make something of ourselves, become doctors, lawyers, senators, editors. All of the role models who visited for News added to the sense that we would have careers."

A segment of the mural

An ambitious mural with a feminist theme in the second-floor hall of the school was designed in 1976 by Art Club students, under the direction of members of the art department. Lucy Mahler, a well-known muralist, was invited to oversee the project. The girls researched the role of women in U.S. history, and made hundreds of sketches before the design was completed. The wall outside the former library (now the Berendsen Room) was measured, gessoed and gridded with chalk lines, while the girls prepared color sketches. Then they transferred the drawings onto the wall with charcoal, and painted the mural itself in acrylic paints. The mural was described in the 1978 issue of the *Alumnae Bulletin:*

> The mural begins with Eve, the first woman and mother of humanity.... In her womb Eve carries two infants arranged in the ancient Chinese yin-yang symbol.
>
> Eve points to a cornucopia of fruit, representing the earth and its abundance. This symbolizes the nurturing aspect of woman and alludes to the role of the American Indian woman and the pioneering woman of our country's infancy.
>
> Out of the mountains behind the cornucopia emerges the strong, intent visage of Harriet Tubman. She points forcefully toward the future, specifically the top of the Capitol building, while below her the Civil War rages.... In the shadow of the seat of government, throngs of immigrant women and suffragettes march out, carrying banners proclaiming the right of women to vote.
>
> The Statue of Liberty is the strongest image in the mural, chosen to symbolize the emerging women of our day. Painted boldly in shades of blue and green, her robes swirl into the sea and onto a road trodden on by a crowd of women to her right.
>
> The Statue of Liberty carries the torch that illuminates the Present, represented by a mother, a scientist, an artist and a welder...
>
> A frieze of faces, intentionally abstract in style, leads toward the Future, where an athlete springs across a bridge. On her back she wears the Chapin wheel and in her hand she carries a diploma.

After many years of featuring creative writing as well as covering aspects of student life, *The Wheel* had become primarily a literary magazine. Later, after 1987, when it joined the Columbia Scholastic Press Association (CSPA), it annually received Columbia's highest Medalist rating, earning praise such as this from judges: "*The Wheel* is a marvelous effort in literary and artistic achievement of the students of The Chapin School. High quality poetry, fiction, and art combine to strengthen the literary/art content. Well designed and visually attractive, the magazine was a delight to read and judge. Congratulations!" The 1999 issue was honored not only with all four CSPA awards (for

Concept, Content, Design and Creativity), but came within six points of a perfect score (of 1000) for excellence.

For some time a publication had been needed that would chronicle student life. The Chapin student newspaper, *Limelight,* made its debut in 1976, covering student concerns as well as outside forces and events. The name *Limelight* was an allusion to the Chapin School colors, green and gold, as well as to the definition of limelight as the focus of public attention. The paper served as a barometer of student opinion on such issues as the dangers of nuclear power, human rights, terrorism and the environment. Two decades later, after consistently earning CSPA awards during the nineties, *Limelight* received the Gold Medalist certificate, CSPA's highest honor. The association commented, "*Limelight* is a very unusual high school paper. It has a spirit of progress and activism shining from its pages.... The talent for writing and the talent for producing the paper comes through to the reader via each page."

The Individual Study Program was introduced in 1977. Class Twelve students submitted proposals for independent study that, once approved, were considered the equivalent of an academic course and evaluated either as Accepted or Not Accepted. The individual study projects were successful and still remain a popular option during the senior year.

Through the years Chapin's faculty has won high praise. Typical alumnae comments were, "The most significant features of my Chapin education were the encouragement and support and genuine caring from the faculty and administration. They're all wonderful!" "My education was so wonderfully well-rounded that my interests draw me toward thousands of different fields.... The intimacy of the classroom setting and the ease of the professor-student relationship are features of my Chapin education that I sorely miss at my university." "The faculty was wonderful. I found that I learned more from some of my teachers at Chapin than I did at college. The study habits instilled at Chapin were extremely important in the study and practice of law. Moreover, the teachers encouraged me to think independently, which is not only unusual but also invaluable."

It was time for a celebration. Under Mrs. Berendsen's leadership, Chapin had weathered the storms of the 1960s, strengthened and adapted the curriculum, renovated and enlarged the school buildings, added a Kindergarten, a Parents' Association and a new state-of-the art library. In September 1975 plans were unveiled for a seventy-fifth birthday party featuring "imaginative, entertaining and festive" anniversary dinners as well as a special Alumnae News Program and a gala Alumnae Luncheon. But new challenges lay ahead, including questions of expansion and accreditation, and the need to further diversify the student body, the faculty and the curriculum.

In 1977 the Board of Trustees, looking toward the future, established a formal Development Office, which after 1978 was under the direction of Virginia Petas for nearly two decades. Plans were made to launch a capital campaign to raise $5 million to endow faculty salaries, scholarships and program enrichment. The campaign was announced in 1981 at Chapin's eightieth birthday parties, two gala dinners at the school, which brought the Chapin family together. As guests arrived, bell-ringers and singers greeted them. Students acted as guides to the different displays and shows in various parts of the building. Displays featured uniforms, photographs of former faculty, and sayings by Lower School students; demonstrations of gymnastics and computer programming were part of the festivities as well. Co-chaired by parents and trustees Elizabeth Brett Webster '58, Cera B. Robbins, and Douglas D. Mercer, the Pledge to the Future campaign exceeded its goal.

In 1978 the Regulations Committee of the Board of Trustees held a meeting to discuss the advantages and disadvantages of accreditation. Until this time the school and others like it had been considered distinguished enough to operate without the process, but now proposed New

The Gordon Room set for the eightieth birthday celebrations, February 1981

Mr. Schrade and the Choral Club at Chapin's eightieth birthday celebration

York State regulations for both public and private schools threatened to impinge on Chapin's academic freedom. Mrs. Berendsen had been worried for some time by the Regents Action Plan, which had authorized the State Department of Education to create curriculum and examinations to which all schools would have to comply. She felt "the plan would have catastrophic results by stifling elements of creativity in both students and teachers as the plan would infringe on about 90 percent of the curriculum."

The tradition continues: Mrs. Berendsen and students wrap Christmas presents for the needy

The Board decided to undergo accreditation. The self-evaluation process by Chapin necessary for accreditation resulted in the preparation of a long-range plan for the school. The evaluation itself, by the New York State Association of Independent Schools (NYSAIS), took place in November 1983, and Chapin was accredited for ten years. The process involved the faculty as well as trustees, staff, parents, alumnae and students. The report of the NYSAIS Accreditation Committee stated, "The Chapin School is obviously one of the strongest schools in the country and is not resting on its laurels, but is continuously looking at itself in a realistic way with an effort to constantly improve." According to NYSAIS regulations, the school would continue to be reevaluated every ten years.

In 1985 an important victory was won by the trustees of NYSAIS, who resolved and affirmed that "accredited schools, having demonstrated their worth through an evaluative process authorized by the Regents, are free to continue without further justification the educational and testing programs they have developed." Schools with membership in NYSAIS were safeguarded by the monitoring of the trustees of the association. Academic freedom was assured if a school presented a brief description of its curriculum, sample examinations and results of standardized testing to the NYSAIS and these met with that association's approval.

On going from the 1960s to the 1970s, Mrs. Berendsen spoke of an evolution "from the nadir of abdication of responsibility…to a new morality…to a greater awareness and appreciation of the special qualities of the school." The transition from the 1970s to the 1980s was less traumatic. In 1980 Jane Walker Garfield '47 became president of Chapin's Board of Trustees. She was the first woman to hold this office since 1929, and the first alumna to be elected president of the Board. For the first time, the Board was under the direction of two women. Phoebe Rentschler Stanton '46 served as chairman from 1969 until 1992. (This position was discontinued in 1997.) Dr. Garfield, looking back on her trusteeship from the vantage point of her fiftieth reunion, remembered it as being relatively problem-free. "We had a financial plan…coeducation was not an issue; our biggest contribution was raising teachers' salaries."

A number of innovations were made at Chapin during the 1980s. New courses and new books were introduced as the curriculum widened and multiculturalism became an intrinsic part of the school's philosophy. Writers Alice Walker and Toni Morrison were added to the syllabus, along with books on feminism and African and Asian history. A Class Three unit on the Vikings was replaced by one on the Mayans. February Week, inaugurated in the seventies, became a time for Upper School students to focus on a particular subject in depth. Science fairs, which continued through the 1990s, were initiated, giving the girls practice in applying the scientific method of investigation. Field trips, which had been part of the students' experience for many years, became an even more integral part of the school's curriculum during the 1980s and 1990s. Class Seven's trip to Boston enhanced their study of American history as did Class Eleven's to Washington, D.C.

Upper School physics and chemistry classes visited the Tokamak Fusion Test Reactor at Princeton University's Plasma Physics Laboratory, and biology classes visited the DNA Learning Center at the Cold Spring Harbor Laboratory on Long Island. Career Day, initiated in 1974, was followed up by more career-oriented activities. A 1982 Faculty Workshop Day focused on the theme "Educating Women for the Future," and in 1985 another faculty workshop, "The Challenge of Stress," took place to "help faculty create a classroom environment sensitive to stress signals given out by students and to heighten awareness of the faculty to the increasing anxiety felt by young women whose options are now unlimited." The demand for guidance increased, and the school responded with more personnel, additional programs and professional consultants. The Alumnae Association, as part of its continuing effort to be a resource for alumnae, sponsored Chapin's first formal Networking Evening in February 1985. One hundred fifty alumnae and a number of mothers of Chapin students joined discussion groups that centered on a wide variety of interests and professions. In 1980, 135 grandparents attended the first Grandparents' Day, now a tradition.

In 1981 members of the Upper School, along with the Advisory Council, organized a program of student interns, whereby students in Classes Ten, Eleven and Twelve would take over classes when teachers knew that they would be away for professional purposes. One faculty member commented, "One of our aims was to lure students into the teaching profession. We were convinced that once they sat in front of a class they'd love it. Our second motive was to show the students that you'll never know anything so well until you teach it."

News, which had formerly either paralyzed or developed a student's speaking abilities, had become a forum for outside speakers, but forensic skills were still emphasized and girls joined the Debating Club, which became the Forensics Club in 1984. After Chapin won the New York State small school championship in 1988, a veteran team member commented, "It is the confidence one gains, the heightened awareness of current events and ability to speak in public that shape the forensic experience."

The scope of the physical education program at the school was broadened when Chapin gained access to such off-campus facilities as the Asphalt Green at Ninetieth Street and York Avenue, a new community center with athletic facilities that eventually included an Olympic-size swimming pool. In 1991 Chapin acquired access to fields on Roosevelt Island as well.

By 1985 the need for additional facilities again became apparent. Mrs. Berendsen spoke of "the absolute necessity of expansion because of the present pressures on the building." Cera B. Robbins had been elected president of the Board of Trustees in 1985, succeeding J. Dennis Delafield. The Trustees planned an expansion, stressing that the goal was to improve the quality of life for the community at Chapin, not to build a larger school for larger numbers of students. Mrs. Berendsen wrote in a brochure sent to parents and alumnae that "the program encompasses adding space to the School affecting three specific areas: the Lower School, science and physical education, and renovating the present building to enhance all disciplines." An $8 million building campaign began in 1986, chaired by parent

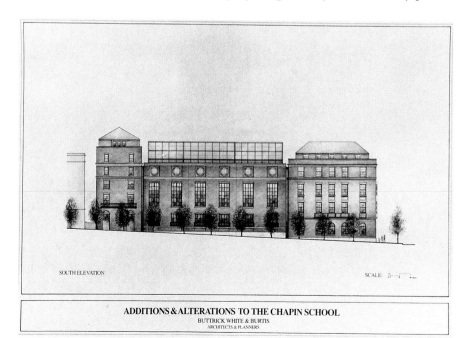

SOUTH ELEVATION

SCALE

ADDITIONS & ALTERATIONS TO THE CHAPIN SCHOOL
BUTTRICK WHITE & BURTIS
ARCHITECTS & PLANNERS

Architectural drawing of proposed alterations, 1987

and trustee Richard J. Schwartz. Once again, the Chapin family responded magnificently—over $9 million was raised.

In 1988 construction began on the new facilities, designed by the architectural firm of Buttrick, White & Burtis. Ruth Proffitt, a 1947 Chapin graduate who returned to the school as a Lower School teacher in 1953, guided the building program. In her forty-six-year career she had served as a room teacher, supervisor, head of Lower and Middle Schools and assistant headmistress for administrative affairs, but she had never before worn a hard hat! Like Miss Jennings, her attention to details, organizational skills and keen insight made her indispensible. Generations of students spoke of her unfailing optimism and ability to make learning fun.

Miss Proffitt in her hard hat

The new facilities reflected changes occurring in women's education, particularly in the sciences. Among the additions were five new laboratory classrooms, a large new gymnasium, a photographic laboratory and carpentry shop, a dance studio, entirely new Lower School classrooms and a resurfaced Gordon Room. The new outdoor play area (on the fourth-floor level) was surfaced with artificial turf. Two new classrooms were created where once there had been a small roof; a faculty lounge and workroom space were carved out of the basement, and the nurse's office was moved to the first floor of the Stringfellow Wing. The official

Volleyball in the new gymnasium

Prayers at the opening of the new space, April 1990

Mr. and Mrs. Berendsen at Smith when Mrs. Berendsen received her honorary degree

opening of the additions and renovations took place on April 13, 1990, when Chapin held an open house to show off its dazzling new space.

By 1992 Mrs. Berendsen had been headmistress for thirty-three years. She seemed in no way diminished by time or responsibility when she advised the Board in May 1992 that she would retire as of June 30, 1993. To many, she *was* the school, generating as much energy as a Con Edison plant.

A student of the 1980s wrote, "When Mrs. Berendsen told us 'someday a woman will be President of the United States, and she just may be sitting in this room,' I believed her. Chapin gave us a singular mission back then: be bold, be brilliant, be original." With a keen awareness of the needs of each generation, Mrs. Berendsen had restructured the curriculum, diversified the student population, and raised faculty salaries. She had been at the forefront of involving the school in the city and beyond, of seeing that the girls had the opportunities to visit with students of other schools, and to take coeducational classes. She had expanded the athletic program, moved the Lower School into a new building, overseen the creation of a computer science department and sanctioned the creation of new science and computer laboratories. During her last years as headmistress, Mrs. Berendsen had targeted the ongoing concerns of the school. She had stressed the importance of continuing to improve communication between the school and parents, students, alumnae and applicants; of keeping Chapin's remarkable faculty happy; of always meeting the needs of individual students and finding ways of providing a broad offering of courses; of accommodating the enlarged physical education program; of providing space for a new library that would be up-to-date technologically, and a renovated Assembly Room that could "better respond to the Drama, Dance and Music Department needs." Through it all she also had counseled parents, mothered students and had taken a personal interest in each staff and faculty member. With a distinctive blend of warmth and authority she had been there to advise and shepherd everyone.

Smith College, her alma mater, had awarded an honorary degree of doctor of humane letters to Mrs. Berendsen in 1991. That same year she

was honored by the Smith College Club of New York at its one hundredth anniversary, when she received the Centennial Honors Award, established to recognize women who "had made a difference." The citation read in part: "In a distinguished career that spans four decades, you continue to set the standard for your profession, yet you remain a pioneer and innovator. As head of one of the finest independent college preparatory schools in the nation, you have not only led your own institution to great academic heights, but have been at the forefront of new initiatives to tackle some of the toughest problems facing education today: serving minority students, attracting and keeping good teachers, breaking down barriers between individual schools."

In notifying the Board of her retirement, Mrs. Berendsen explained that the school was in a strong position academically, the preliminary reports for the Evaluation Committee for the New York State Association of Independent Schools, scheduled to arrive in October 1993, were being written, and the building had been renovated. The time was right for someone new to come in and lead Chapin into the twenty-first century. A search for the next head of school began that summer.

Members of the Board commended Mrs. Berendsen. Harry Havemeyer, parent of six Chapin daughters and trustee emeritus, wrote "Character, integrity, good judgment—when I think of Millie Berendsen I think of these. During the ten years that I was President of the Board of Trustees I never once saw her make a decision that did not turn out to be the right one for Chapin. Millie's judgment about deci-

Mrs. Berendsen

Brearley's tribute to Mrs. Berendsen

sions and the timing of them has been faultless. As the ancient prayer says, 'holding fast to that which is good,' and at the same time changing to meet legitimate new needs for a new generation, along that thin line, sometimes almost invisible, Millie has led Chapin with distinction." Cera Robbins praised her, "It is hard to put into words Millie's extraordinary contribution to Chapin and education in general, but the citation from Smith says it well. Begin with these well-deserved tributes, add a large measure of humor, compassion, integrity, strength, wisdom and energy, and a great singing voice—stir well—and you may be getting close to the essence of our Millie: a truly remarkable woman and an amazing friend." And one teacher praised the headmistress in the October 1992 issue of *Limelight:* "Mrs. Berendsen has avoided fads and trends, while keeping up with or even being ahead of the times. Hers is a measured and carefully thought-out approach to education."

From the students there were tributes, too: albums of pictures, poems and stories, a video of her life, a puppet show and a table inlaid with tiles, one designed by each class, with the wheel emblem in the center. In recognition of her love of music, the faculty and staff gave a sound system. And she received citations from President Bill Clinton, Governor Mario Cuomo and Mayor David Dinkins.

At their annual luncheon in April 1993, Chapin alumnae honored her. Alumnae representing eight decades spoke eloquently about Mrs. Berendsen and the school. The Alumnae Association gave her a gold wheel pin as well as a hooked rug depicting students at Prayers. To reflect her athletic interests, the next present was a sports outfit. Perhaps the most precious gift to the headmistress was that she was declared an honorary alumna of the school, Class of 1945.

Brearley, a friend and rival through all the years, sent a poem written by a Brearley trustee, along with a check for $10,000 to Chapin in Mrs. Berendsen's honor.

In May, parents of alumnae came to a reception for Mrs. Berendsen, and all trustees who had ever served with her were invited to a dinner in her honor. There the Board of Trustees

Mr. and Mrs. Berendsen with Ms. Theunick

presented her with a bowl inscribed with the Chapin wheel. The evening's entertainment was a hilarious series of skits about Mrs. Berendsen's time at Chapin.

A magnificent tribute to Mrs. Berendsen came in the form of a proposal by the Annenberg Foundation. Ambassador and Mrs. Walter Annenberg, Chapin grandparents, challenged the school to raise $3 million for a Mildred Jeanmaire Berendsen Endowment Fund, honoring her thirty-four years of "exceptional leadership and dedication to Chapin." If the challenge were met, the foundation would contribute $1 million. The fund would be used for faculty salaries, scholarships and program enhancement and was nicknamed "Millions for Millie." The challenge was not only met, but exceeded.

On learning of her retirement, tributes poured in from alumnae: "The most vivid memory among Chapin young alumnae was that Mrs. Berendsen knew each girl's name." "She evoked the perfect combination of fear, discipline, enthusiasm, respect and intellectual curiosity in all of us." And last, the memory of a touching moment from a student who had decided to leave Chapin to attend another school: "Mrs. Berendsen exclaimed: 'Just remember, no matter where you go, you will always be a Chapin girl.'"

CHAPTER SIX

PREPARING FOR
A NEW CENTURY

*In this particular school, young women have been taught
from Miss Chapin's time up to the present day that the best
way to make your way is together — through relationships
that foster independence through interdependence.*

SANDRA THEUNICK
HEAD OF SCHOOL, 1993–

*S*andra Theunick's appointment as Chapin's new head of school was
unanimously approved by the Board of Trustees on March 29, 1993,
after an extensive search involving trustees, faculty, staff, parents and
alumnae. Mrs. Berendsen enthusiastically endorsed the choice, commenting that she could now leave the school knowing it was in good
hands.

In Ms. Theunick the school found a head who was known and
respected at the national level. Born in Michigan, Ms. Theunick had
graduated from the Stone Ridge School in Washington, D.C., and
received a B.A. in psychology from Newton College of the Sacred
Heart, a women's college in Boston. She had completed advanced certi-
fication in Mental Health Studies at Georgetown University and earned
a master's degree in divinity at Washington Theological Union.

The Annenberg Center for Learning and Research

Ms. Theunick

Ms. Theunick had spent her entire career as an educator. Her work as a member of the Religious of the Sacred Heart—a teaching order of the Catholic Church—had provided unique and invaluable training. She rose to the position of head of the Forest Ridge School in Bellevue, Washington, and then head of Stuart Country Day School in Princeton, New Jersey. Both are all-girl schools encompassing elementary and secondary education. At the time she came to Chapin, she was chair of the School Heads Advisory Committee of the National Association of Independent Schools, and chair of the Trustee Committee of the New Jersey Association of Independent Schools. Later, she became chair of the Council for Spiritual and Ethical Education, a national organization that focuses on moral, ethical and spiritual education for independent schools.

A warm, caring person with extraordinary energy, Ms. Theunick said at the outset, "My door is aways open." Described by a colleague as "a generous spirit," her thoughtfulness has been evidenced many times over in her concern for faculty, staff and students. With a strong sense of community, she, like her predecessors, considered everyone associated with the school as part of a family. She gained a larger family of her own, including both daughters and granddaughters, upon her marriage to Dennis Arthur Fisher in 1999.

Ms. Theunick fit the splendid mold of her predecessors with her deep commitment to women's education, her love of teaching, her ethical principles and educational goals, her exuberance and fine intelligence. At the same time she represented a new model of leadership. She urged the entire community "to be shareholders in the life of Chapin." She had always built her administrative structure around strong support, encouraging people to work together and communicate effectively to solve problems. Delegating for Ms. Theunick exemplified a way of caring, caring that all people grow in their ability to take on responsibility. She considered it critical for the ongoing success of the school to regard faculty and staff as partners in a common endeavor. She thought that Prayers should reflect the increasingly diverse backgrounds of the current student body and wanted to develop adult leadership by involving more people in setting a direction for the school. At all times she stressed putting the girls first. "The world expects more and more of its women," she said, "and Chapin girls, as citizens of the world, should be ready to face any challenge."

Students referred to Ms. Theunick as "a good role model," "inspiring," and "very responsive." Believing that it was important to teach—"to keep up with the pulse of the girls"—she continued her predecessors' tradition of teaching classes, including a course in public speaking to Class Eight and an elective in comparative religion to Upper School students. "Her expectations are high," one student commented. A wonderful sense of humor helped her to deal effectively with everyday challenges. "She's very funny," one student commented. A colleague described her as "a woman of substance," noting her dependability, and added, "she can laugh at herself."

Believing that "the job of head is to be able to stand apart from the institution and be its best friend and most loyal critic," Ms. Theunick studied her new school, and in November of her first year, told the Board what she saw as her greatest challenges. She wanted to enrich the quality of student life through social and coeducational opportunities, as well as through community service. She wanted to introduce a life-skills program that would help students make good decisions and develop leadership abilities, and she saw an increased need for psychological support services. Enrollment, fund-raising, changes to the physical plant, and helping and evaluating faculty and staff were also stressed. As a result, a strategic plan took shape to help Chapin define its goals for the twenty-first century.

This plan reflected Ms. Theunick's background in education and addressed issues of continuing concern. The strategic planning process, chaired by trustee Patty Murphy Paine '55, formally began in February 1996. The school drew upon the ideas and advice of past and present heads of school, trustees, parents, grandparents, alumnae, faculty, staff and students. The planning effort called upon many members of the community to assume increased leadership roles, reinforcing Ms. Theunick's egalitarian philosophy, and her desire to foster a willingness to accept both risks and responsibility.

The Strategic Goals for 1997–2007 were defined in a booklet entitled *Chapin Meets the Future*. Two of Chapin's most enduring goals—maintaining a strong academic program and a fine faculty—were understandably given priority. The changing times dictated the importance of creating a more multicultural community so that Chapin could continue to attract the best minds among the increasingly diverse young women of

New York City. The life-skills program would nurture the education of the whole person and teach young women how to handle situations related to urban safety and family problems that they could encounter in life. The program's emphasis on leadership, moral and ethical development, responsible citizenship and health and well-being stressed the aims of Ms. Theunick and reflected those of Miss Chapin as well. Several years after the program was established, Ms. Theunick could say, "I think my strength has been to keep us independent in terms of social striving, not prey to adult peer pressure." Other goals were to keep abreast of technology and to maintain a physical plant with superior facilities.

To achieve all these goals, in 1997 the school embarked on the Chapin Centennial Campaign, co-chaired by Chapin parents and trustees Mary Gordon Roberts '56 and Dorothy Whitmarsh Sprague '74. With a goal of $30 million, the aims of the campaign were to provide for new building and renovations, including funding for technology, and to increase the school's endowment for the purposes of maintaining competitive faculty compensation and supporting financial aid. New facilities, designed by the firm of Butler Rogers Baskett and added as a result of this campaign, included a library/multimedia center, a dining room, a gymnasium, a kindergarten room, a black box theater, a greenhouse, and a play roof. A new climate-controlled archives room replaced the school's former repository for Chapin's documents and artifacts of historical interest.

Many years of thought and planning culminated in an extraordinary new library facility made possible by the generosity of Ambassador and Mrs. Walter H. Annenberg. The Annenberg Center for Learning and Research, completed in 1998, is a 10,000-square-foot facility for the Lower, Middle and Upper Schools, located in the center of the school on the fourth- and fifth-floor levels. It has all the technological capability of a modern library, including a multimedia classroom and the capacity for over 50,000 volumes. Books are housed on movable stacks with ample space for the collections to grow. An art and music alcove, equipped with stereos, CD players and headphones, houses the school's fine-art reference books and music collection.

Until the Gordon Room was redesigned, it served both as the school's dining area and as a gymnasium. Now the Gordon Room is a community center—where students, teachers and staff can meet spontaneously during the day. The completely renovated kitchen offers a wide array of nutritional choices, illustrating in a domestic way the changes the school and its community have undergone since Miss

The Annenberg Center

Chapin's days. Since 1980 the cafeteria has been operated by a food service. The Chapin lunch in the late 1990s features many ethnic dishes, a wide range of vegetarian choices, homemade soups, a salad bar and an ice-cream case stocked with delectables twice a week. The new cafeteria, open from 7:30 A.M. to 5:00 P.M., also provides a continental breakfast and snacks all day. A Chapin girl's predilection for sweets remains undiminished. A recent alumna remembered her classmates daring each other to sneak back into the kitchen to get more cookies and the stern edict from behind the cafeteria counter: "Just one dessert, girls!"

To replace the space formerly used in the Gordon Room for physical activity, a gymnasium was built on the sixth floor above the Annenberg Center. The gym is large enough to include regulation courts for volleyball and badminton and provides an appropriate court size for Middle School basketball games. Seventy-seven percent of the girls from Classes Seven to Twelve were on a team by the 1990s, with varsity and junior varsity teams playing twenty-two different sports.

A strong dramatics program has always been a part of the Chapin curriculum, but in recent years the school has not had enough space to accommodate the program. Drama classes and rehearsals occurred in whatever space was available on a day-to-day basis—from the Assembly Room to a gym, a random classroom to a corridor. Sets and lights could

Keeping abreast of technology

not be installed until a few days before a performance and had to be taken down immediately. Now, to the delight of all thespians, a 1,600-square-foot black box theater personally tailored to Chapin's cast and crew has been constructed on the sixth floor above the library. The lighting pipes are hung low enough for a Class Nine student to reach without a ladder. The theater is used for classes during the day, workshops with guest artists and for technical work and rehearsals after school and on the weekends.

In addition to these major projects, Chapin recently expanded the technology facilities for the Middle and Upper School computer laboratories, added a new kindergarten to provide smaller class groupings and created a computer workroom, adjacent to the student lounge, for Class Twelve. Five other areas were moved and rebuilt: the outdoor play deck, the choral room (named for Charles Dodsley Walker), the ceramics and woodworking classrooms, the business and development offices and the greenhouse. The greenhouse replaced the original built by Miss Fairfax in 1928. For fifty years or more, every girl who came for an interview received a plant from the greenhouse, and, if she became a Chapin student, learned her first botany lessons there. The tradition continues. One plant presented to an entrant lived long enough to participate in a Williams College education! One science teacher commented, "I don't have to worry about the girls getting splinters from chips in the slate tops. Not only is it aesthetically beautiful, it's also the safest greenhouse." Another said, "It's the most exhilarating place in which to teach. It has a great river view, it's quiet, and it's spacious.... I would not have a botany program for our seventh-graders if it weren't for the new greenhouse." Miss Fairfax would approve.

In talking with the Class of 1997, whose parents donated their class gift to the publication of this history, differences and similarities between the Chapin girls of today and those of yesteryear became apparent.

In appearance, the 1997 student bore little resemblance to her demure predecessor in green serge. More casually clad and relaxed in manner, she came across as assertive and outspoken. Her choice of

The greenhouse, 1999

career was of paramount importance. Marriage and children were not yet goals. "We don't even think about it." If the Class of 1917 looked up to boys, it's safe to say the Class of 1997 felt at least equal to them.

Happily, many links to the past were unbroken. The girls felt they had been given a superior education. Fresh air, sunshine, gymnastics and the playing field were still an integral part of school life. Their commitment to community service was firmly entrenched. Like the early Chapinites, they were proud of their school, of its facilities and pleasant atmosphere. Chapin was a safe haven. A student declared, "The school is like Fort Knox." After the death of her father, one member of Class Twelve commented, "I couldn't have been in a better place. Everyone was there for me, and the faculty was so supportive I couldn't have coped without them." Another student dropped French after Class Ten and took ancient Greek. "I'm the only one. If you want to do something, at Chapin they accommodate you."

Thanksgiving Prayers, 1997

One student discerned the following themes in her schoolmates' Chapin experiences of the 1990s: "Courage, commitment, cooperation, confidence and camaraderie. What struck me is that much of what is identified as Chapinesque is by no means unique to our time at school. Instead many of these themes have existed since Chapin's foundation." She might have added "community," a theme stressed by all of Chapin's headmistresses. Sandra Theunick wrote, "Chapin is a school in which great efforts are made by individuals to pay attention to common good."

Miss Chapin would be pleased with the school's splendid new facilities. She would also be proud to see her ideas and values still emphasized and taught in faculty-student get-togethers, classrooms and in Prayers, still a spiritual forum, now more reflective of the broad scope of traditions represented in the current student body. She would be quick to commend the legions of Upper School girls who continue to be involved in community service and, surely, as a visionary and pioneer she would approve of Chapin's culturally diverse curriculum and the broad spectrum of cultures and backgrounds represented by the students, faculty and staff. She would also approve of her successor Sandra Theunick, who supported not only increased diversity but also the inclusive environment in which it could thrive. A visionary herself,

Ms. Theunick wanted to create a world that would be, in her words, "a safe, yet challenging place" for the children of different cultures and spiritual beliefs in her care. She will be remembered for the warmth and determination with which she continued to address the whole issue of diversity and for recognizing the truth of Bishop Lawrence's words, written in 1927: "Able and intellectual children from different groups are essential to a good school.... The segregation of any one class is fatal to the rounded education of that class."

Ms. Theunick with students

Chapin has been blessed with exceptional headmistresses. The excellence of its education rivals that of any college preparatory institution in the country. The atmosphere of the school is warm and courteous, and the building itself is beautiful. The elusive qualities of good manners and of grace still prevail. The issue of racial and ethnic diversity among both the faculty and students is being thoughtfully addressed, and the goals outlined in the strategic planning process are being pursued and met. For seventy-five years the Board of Trustees, with clarity of vision and financial acuity, has successfully guided the school so that each generation could, in Miss Chapin's words, "welcome the future with joyful, enthusiastic acceptance of its new opportunities."

Change is necessary for growth, and the school has navigated the waves of history, strengthening and adapting its curriculum and its institutions through the years. Even as the twentieth century saw incredible social and technological change, the spirit of the great educators who have guided Chapin has remained constant. The words of Barnard's Dean Gildersleeve are as relevant today as they were in 1928, when she spoke at the dedication of 100 East End Avenue. "This is a good school," she said. "I have long thought of it as one of the pillars of women's education in New York City, a firm foundation on which to build the higher structure of college and university. The school has been, like so many of our best institutions, the flowering of one vigorous personality and the associates she has gathered around her."

May the school forever sustain Dean Gildersleeve's 1928 vision of Chapin as a "glowing star, perpetually reborn, radiating forth always from these halls new energy, new life, new light."

FROM THE AUTHOR

When I set out to write a history of Chapin I did not attempt to be scholarly, but I tried to be accurate and logical. I wanted to tell the story of a great school by concentrating on the personalities that forged it and, peripherally, the forces that shaped the twentieth century. I knew that this loose assortment of anecdotes and snippets of historical matter could include irrelevant information while omitting important facts. My first object was to write something readable. I wanted to convey the flavor and special charm of Chapin. One feels the unique atmosphere of the school as soon as one enters its door. It can no longer be characterized as an old-world elegance, for Chapin is a thoroughly modern school, poised to cut sleekly through the waves of the twenty-first century. Yet an aura of courtesy, of certitude and of calm prevails. How that aura was created and how it has been preserved provided the impetus for this anecdotal history.

Charlotte Johnson Noerdlinger '51

ACKNOWLEDGMENTS

We acknowledge with appreciation the generosity of the parents of the Class of 1997, who donated their Class Twelve gift toward the publication of this book. Every effort has been made to be accurate; however, any history is only as good as its sources. We thank all contributors to this history. At the same time we note with regret that lacunae may have created imbalances. A bouquet of thanks to the faculty, staff and students who cheerfully submitted to being interviewed and who gave much wonderful information. A special thank you to all alumnae, parents and trustees whose stories and pictures enliven the history, and to the noble souls who worked with this book in all its stages, helping to make it accurate, aesthetically pleasing and coherent: Barbara Belknap '51, Mildred Berendsen, Frances Bloom, Louise Belknap Carter '45, Gerard Chamorin, Dana Cole, Elie de Comminges, Cathy Dorsey, Dianne Dyslin, Marion Eaton, Ella Foshay '65, Celia Fuller, Christopher Gray, Terry Gumz, Louise Henderson, Peggy High '55, Don Kennison, Laura Lindgren, Katharine Walker MacKenty '23, Mark Magowan, Duane Neil, Patty Murphy Paine '55, Virginia Petas, Philip Reynolds, Cera Robbins, Henry Schiavone, Elaine Stainton, Sandra Theunick, Benjamin Tripp, Spencer Vining and Mary Norman Whiteside. We appreciate being able to draw on Chapin publications and reports as well as on the following publications for information and quotations: *A History of a Young Ladies School,* by Mary Anthony and Grace Chapin; *The Sixties — Days of Hope, Days of Rage,* by Todd Gitlin; *Town and Country* magazine, for the article "Growing Up Then" by Sarah Ann Dinkins Britton '54; and *Avenue* magazine for articles by Christopher Gray. Our appreciation also goes to Carol Bates, Dan Budnik, Michael Sherman, Martha McKeen Welch, Elsie Trask Wheeler '50, Linda Williams, Culver Pictures, Inc., the New-York Historical Society and the New York Public Library for their photographs, and to Holley Wall Flagg '58 for the painting on the book's cover.

Most of all, thanks to Eleanor Southworth, guardian of the archives, who encouraged and guided the author from day one. Her ability to pull out the necessary material, to answer all questions and to help focus on what was important was of incalculable value. Her penchant for nonstop hard work and accuracy are exceeded only by her integrity, kindness and grace.

1901   Maria Bowen Chapin establishes Miss Chapin's School for Girls and Kindergarten for Boys and Girls at 12 West Forty-seventh Street with seven teachers and seventy-eight students.

1905   The school moves to 46 and 48 East Fifty-eighth Street.

1908   The first diplomas are awarded.

1909   Self-Government begins.

1910   The school moves to 32 and 34 East Fifty-seventh Street.

1911   Miss Chapin and Miss Mary Cecelia Fairfax form a partnership "for the conduct in the City of New York of the school for girls and young children heretofore carried on by Miss Chapin." ◆ The school is now known as Miss Chapin's School for Girls. ◆ The Athletic Association is formed.

1912   The first Field Day is held. Field Day was held at Hartsdale until 1927. After 1927, Field Day was held successively at the Scarborough School, the Riverdale Country School, Randall's Island, and Bear Mountain.

1913   Miss Fairfax becomes associate headmistress. ◆ The first formal commencement is held.

1914   The Alumnae Association is formed by Miss Chapin to do war and welfare work. ◆ The uniform is introduced.

1917   The last year that boys are included in the school. ◆ The first issue of *The Wheel* is printed.

1919   The Club formally organizes.

1920   The Dramatic Club is organized.

1922   The Audubon Club is organized.

1924   The Choral Club is organized.

1925   The school is incorporated as Miss Chapin's School, Ltd. ◆ Twenty-three diplomas are awarded. The enrollment is 319 students.

1927   Funds are raised for a new school building at Eighty-fourth Street and East End Avenue. This first major fund-raising effort is known as The Building Fund of Miss Chapin's School, Ltd.

1928   The school moves to a new building at 100 East End Avenue. ◆ The Kindergarten is discontinued.

1932   Miss Chapin retires from active management of the school. ◆ Ethel Grey Stringfellow becomes joint headmistress with Miss Fairfax.

1934   According to Miss Chapin's wish, the name of the school is changed to The Chapin School, Ltd. ◆ Death of Miss Chapin on March 8.

1935   Death of Miss Fairfax on February 28. ◆ Miss Stringfellow becomes headmistress. ◆ The Alumnae Association is reorganized.

1936   The original uniform, dating back to 1914, is updated to a new style and remains the same until 1971.

1937   The first Alumnae Luncheon is given. ◆ The first issue of *The Cog* is printed.

1939   The Dancing Club is organized.

1943   The Chapin-Brearley Exchange, an exchange for children's clothing, sporting equipment and books, is founded. With money raised through this service the Exchange contributes to the scholarship funds of the Chapin and Brearley Schools.

1945   Self-Government is extended to the Middle School.

1946   *The Chapin School Alumnae Bulletin* is published in its present format.

1949   Chapin becomes a charter member of the Alumnae Presidents' Council of Independent Schools. This organization, now the Alumni Program Council, is a resource for alumni associations as well as alumni and staff of member schools all over the country.

1951   Chapin's fiftieth anniversary. The school's enrollment is 400 students.

1957   The Guaranty Fund drive is begun to raise $1,000,000 for faculty pensions and salaries. When completed, the sum of $1,375,000 is the largest amount ever raised by a girls' day school. ◆ Annual Giving is established.

1959   Miss Stringfellow retires after fifty years at Chapin (three years as joint headmistress, twenty-four as headmistress). ◆ Mildred Jeanmaire Berendsen becomes headmistress.

1963   The Ethel Grey Stringfellow Art Case is given by alumnae in honor of Miss Stringfellow. ◆ Alumnae tours and trips begin. ◆ The first issue of *The Chapin School Newsletter* is published.

1968   The Development Fund, with a goal of $2,500,000, is started to raise funds for faculty salaries and building enlargement.

1969   Ground breaking takes place for a new wing of the school. ◆ 535 East 84 Street, the building adjacent to 100 East End Avenue, becomes available. The decision is made to purchase the building rather than to build a new wing. This building is named the Ethel

Grey Stringfellow Wing. • The Parents' Association is founded and provides a wide variety of extracurricular activities for students.

1970   Death of Miss Stringfellow on May 8.

1971   The Interschool Program, now composed of Brearley, Browning, Chapin, Collegiate, Dalton, Nightingale-Bamford, Spence and Trinity schools, is established to provide expanded opportunities for students in curricular and extracurricular areas. • A new uniform is introduced.

1972   Renovation of the Ethel Grey Stringfellow Wing is completed. • The Ethel Grey Stringfellow Library is dedicated.

1973   The Chapin-Brearley Academic Exchange is established, permitting girls in both schools to take courses offered by Chapin or Brearley alone.

1974   The Kindergarten is reintroduced.

1975   Chapin's seventy-fifth anniversary is celebrated,
TO   highlighted by three gala dinners at the school for
1976   the entire Chapin family and an alumnae show about Chapin's history. • The first issue of *Limelight,* the student newspaper, is published. • The school's enrollment is 560 students.

1977   The Individual Studies Program, an opportunity for independent study/projects, is initiated for members of Class Twelve.

1979   The Endowment Fund drive, with a goal of $5,000,000, is begun to raise funds for faculty salaries, scholarships and enrichment programs.

1981   Chapin's eightieth anniversary celebrations: the entire Chapin family is invited to two festive dinners at the school as the final phase of The Endowment Fund drive is launched. • The Mary Rousmaniere Gordon Room is dedicated.

1984   Chapin is accredited by The New York State Association of Independent Schools.

1986   Building for the Future, a capital campaign to raise $8,000,000 for improvement and expansion of the school's facilities, is organized.

1987   Construction of a gymnasium and outdoor sports
TO   area takes place, as well as a new Lower School area,
1990   science and art facilities and the redesign and renovation of other spaces in the school.

1992   A challenge grant of $1,000,000 to establish The Mildred Jeanmaire Berendsen Endowment Fund is offered to Chapin by the Annenberg Foundation.

1993   Mrs. Berendsen retires after forty-four years at Chapin (thirty-four as headmistress). • Sandra J. Theunick becomes head of school.

1994   Chapin meets the Annenberg Challenge. The Mildred Jeanmaire Berendsen Endowment Fund exceeds $4,500,000.

1996   A major strategic planning initiative, including trustees, alumnae, parents, faculty and students, is begun to evaluate long-range goals for Chapin.

1997   The Chapin-Brearley Exchange is closed after fifty-four years of raising funds for the scholarship programs of the Chapin and Brearley Schools. • The Chapin Centennial Campaign is initiated to raise $30,000,000 for facilities and technology, faculty compensation, financial aid and facility and program maintenance.

1998   Completion and dedication of all new spaces, including the Annenberg Center for Learning and Research, highlighted by two gala dinner celebrations at the school for the entire Chapin family with demonstrations by Upper School students.

2000   Chapin begins its one-hundredth-anniversary cele-
TO   brations by launching its web site and printing *And*
2001   *Cheer for the Green and Gold: An Anecdotal History of The Chapin School.* • The centennial year begins with a party at the Museum of the City of New York, followed by an evening of master classes, an alumnae panel addressing "The Challenges of the 21st Century," a retrospective show and a centennial benefit at Randall's Island with fireworks to end the yearlong celebration. • Enrollment is 660 students.

PRESIDENTS OF SELF-GOVERNMENT

1909–1910	Helen Dunscombe Auerbach	1955–1956	Llewellyn Swayne Parsons
1910–1911	Lois Scott Hall	1956–1957	Sarah Flanagan Gordon
1911–1912	Mary Baker	1957–1958	Louise Parsons
1912–1913	Louise Moore Herrick	1958–1959	Ellen Zinsser McCloy
1913–1914	Josephine de Gersdorff	1959–1960	Isabella Macomb Edwards
1914–1915	Alma de Gersdorff	1960–1961	Dorothy Page Schneirla
1915–1916	Helen Hoadley	1961–1962	Vivienne Yu
1916–1917	Theodora Mead	1962–1963	Mary Ann Delafield Cox
1917–1918	Eleanor Erving King	1963–1964	Susannah Hendricks Wood
1918–1919	Helen Rice	1964–1965	Deborah Anne Randall
1919–1920	Marion Taylor	1965–1966	Darcy Brisbane Kelley
1920–1921	Rosamond Borland	1966–1967	Leslie Conover Wilson
1921–1922	Augusta Webb Trimble	1967–1968	Ann–Woodson Ramsey
1922–1923	Emily Delafield Floyd	1968–1969	Elizabeth Hamilton Munnell
1923–1924	Anne Spencer Morrow	1969–1970	Melissa Carow Jackson
1924–1925	Martha Rosalie Humphrey	1970–1971	Coline Elizabeth Covington
1925–1926	Mary Willis Swords	1971–1972	Jane Marie Doyle
1926–1927	Blanchette Ferry Hooker	1972–1973	Caroline Anne Ryan
1927–1928	Mary Farwell Rousmaniere	1973–1974	Dorothy Sutton Whitmarsh
1928–1929	Rosilla Marshall Hornblower	1974–1975	Deirdre Elyse Bradley
1929–1930	Hester Livingstone Adams	1975–1976	Jacqueline Kate Nash
1930–1931	Hope Brown	1976–1977	Esmé Cogswell Murphy
1931–1932	Laura Guy French	1977–1978	Aleta Nicholson Murphy
1932–1933	Ruth Hilda Holmes	1978–1979	Evalyn Brooke Lee
1933–1934	Mabel Brady Garvan	1979–1980	Andrea Blaugrund
1934–1935	Elizabeth Hedwig Mason	1980–1981	Rorianne Cassandra Schrade
1935–1936	Cynthia Lenox Banks	1981–1982	Katharine Blair Williams
1936–1937	Constance Hoyt	1982–1983	Caroline Young
1937–1938	Isabel Stettinius Marsh	1983–1984	Zelda Samara Owens
1938–1939	Margot Damrosch Finletter	1984–1985	Robin Lynn Silverman
1939–1940	Monica Wyatt	1985–1986	Jane Dora Hearst
1940–1941	Julia May Richmond	1986–1987	Patricia Anne Haldi
1941–1942	Ann Welling	1987–1988	Jennifer Noelle Collet
1942–1943	Cristobel Locke	1988–1989	Alexandra Warner Cole
1943–1944	Virginia Moffat	1989–1990	Melissa Ashley Chang
1944–1945	Helen Anderton	1990–1991	Sarah Densen Baden
1945–1946	Louise Harding Earle	1991–1992	Katharine Howell Brandi
1946–1947	Betty Franklin Palmedo	1992–1993	Ruby Nueki Anyimi
1947–1948	Julia Nicholson Beals	1993–1994	Katherine B. Lane
1948–1949	Elizabeth Anne Fitz Randolph	1994–1995	Neylan McBaine
1949–1950	Katharine Hamlin Edgar	1995–1996	Kadija Ferryman
1950–1951	Susan Helen Rentschler	1996–1997	Valerie Sinckler
1951–1952	Charlotte Alison Smith	1997–1998	Linda T. Munro
1952–1953	Mildred Machado	1998–1999	Elizabeth K. Kelly
1953–1954	Constance Ludington Brown	1999–2000	Elizabeth Lithgow Olive
1954–1955	Moira Cameron MacVeagh	2000–2001	Aidan Christine O'Connor

THE CHAPIN SCHOOL DATES

(REVISED IN 1975)

B.C.

c. 3000 Pyramid Age began
First Calendar in Egypt

c. 1720 Hammurabi's Code of Laws
in Babylon

c. 1600 Golden Age of Cretan
Civilization

1000 David, King of the Hebrews

c. 800 Homer and the *Iliad*

c. 776 The First Olympiad

753 Rome founded

621 The Deuteronomic Code of
the Hebrews

612 Nineveh destroyed by Medes
and Chaldeans

586 Fall of Jerusalem

c. 563 Birth of Buddha

551 Birth of Confucius

550 Croesus, King of Lydia

510 Expulsion of Kings from
Rome
Establishment of Roman
Republic

490 Battle of Marathon

480 Battles of Thermopolae and
Salamis

c. 445 Periclean Age

404 End of the Peloponnesian
Wars

399 Death of Socrates

323 Death of Alexander the Great
Hellenistic Age

218 Hannibal crossed the Alps

55 Caesar invaded Britain

31 Battle of Actium

27 Augustan Age
Beginning of the Roman
Empire

A.D.

70 Siege of Jerusalem by Titus

79 Destruction of Pompeii and
Herculaneum

180 Death of Marcus Aurelius
End of Pax Romana

325 First Council of Nicaea

378 Battle of Adrianople

410 Alaric, the Goth, took Rome

440 Pope Leo I, the Great

450 Conquest of Britain by
Angles and Saxons

451 Battle of Châlons

476 Fall of the Roman Empire in
the West

496 Conversion of Clovis to
Orthodox Christianity

526 St. Benedict's Rule

597 St. Augustine sent to England
by Pope Gregory I, the Great

622 The Hegira

664 Synod of Whitby—brought
Church of England under
supervision of Church
of Rome

732 Battle of Tours

752 Pippin crowned King of the
Franks by St. Boniface

800 Charlemagne crowned
Emperor of the West by Pope
Leo III

899 Death of Alfred the Great

962 Otto I crowned Holy Roman
Emperor

987 Hugh Capet in France

1066 Norman Conquest of England

1077 Henry IV submitted to
Gregory VII at Canossa

1096 First Crusade
Pope Urban II

1188 Third Crusade
Richard I of England
Philip II of France
Frederick I of Germany
Yoritomo, First Shogun of
Japan

1210 St. Francis and Innocent III

1215 Magna Carta

1250 Death of Frederick II

1280 Kublai Khan, Mongol ruler
of China. Marco Polo

1295 Model Parliament under
Edward I

1300 Dante's *Divine Comedy*

1302 Commons or Third Estate
called to Estates General by
Philip IV of France

1337 Death of Giotto

1346 Battle of Crécy at the
beginning of the Hundred
Years' War

1377 End of the Babylonian
Captivity of the Church
Beginning of the Great
Schism

1381 John Wyclif
Peasants' Revolt in England

1414 Council of Constance

1415 Burning of John Huss
Battle of Agincourt

1431 Burning of Joan of Arc

1453 End of the Hundred Years'
War
Constantinople taken by the
Turks
Fall of the Eastern Empire

1456 Bible printed at Mainz by
John Gutenberg

1492 Columbus discovered the
New World
Moors expelled from Spain
Death of Lorenzo de' Medici

1497 John Cabot claimed North
America for England

1519 Emporer Charles V, Henry
VIII, Francis I, Pope Leo X
Death of Leonardo da Vinci
Beginning of Magellan's
voyage

1521 Edict of Worms outlawed
Luther

1538 Order of Jesuits established
by Ignatius Loyola

1543 Copernicus published his
theory of the solar system

1564 Death of Michelangelo

1568	Rebellion of The Netherlands against Philip II of Spain led by William the Silent of Orange	1806	Holy Roman Empire dissolved	1917	The United States declared war against Germany
1572	Massacre of St. Bartholomew's Day	1807	Robert Fulton's steamboat in the United States		Fall of the Russian Empire and establishment of the Soviet State
1588	Spanish Armada Elizabeth of England Philip of Spain	1813	Richard Wagner born	1918	Armistice signed
		1815	Battle of Waterloo		Fall of the German and Austrian Empires
1598	Edict of Nantes issued by Henry IV of France	1822	Louis Pasteur born	1919	League of Nations established
1607	Settlement of Jamestown	1825	Locomotive invented by George Stephenson in England	1927	Lindbergh's nonstop solo flight to France
1614	First settlement on Manhattan	1831	Michael Faraday discovered principle for electric generator	1929	Stock Market panic in Wall Street
1616	Death of Shakespeare	1848	European revolutions		Vatican City established as a sovereign state by Pope Pius XI and Mussolini
1642	Civil War in England Death of Galileo Birth of Sir Isaac Newton		Second French Republic End of war between United States and Mexico Karl Marx—*Communist Manifesto*	1931	Japan took Manchuria
1644	Antonio Stradivari born: perfected the violin			1935	Italy attacked Ethiopia
1648	Treaty of Westphalia at the end of the Thirty Years' War about Religion	1852	Second French Empire: Napoleon III	1937	Japan invaded China
		1853	Beginning of Crimean War	1939	World War II began with Hitler's attack on Poland
1649	Execution of Charles I	1859	Charles Darwin—*The Origin of Species*	1940	Winston Churchill, British Prime Minister
1685	Johann Sebastian Bach born: polyphonic writing Edict of Nantes revoked by Louis XIV	1861	Alexander II freed the serfs in Russia Kingdom of Italy founded under Victor Emmanuel	1941	Japanese surprise attack on Pearl Harbor
1687	Newton formulated the laws of gravitation	1861–65	Civil War in the United States	1942	First nuclear-controlled chain reaction—University of Chicago
1688	Glorious Revolution in England: James II, William III and Mary	1870	Franco-Prussian War Third Republic in France End of Temporal Power of the Pope	1945	Atomic bomb dropped on Hiroshima and Nagasaki End of World War II United Nations Charter drawn up at San Francisco
1713	Treaty of Utrecht at the end of the War of the Spanish Succession	1871	German Empire united under William I of Prussia Bismarck	Since 1945	Decline of overseas empires and formation of independent nations in Africa and Asia
1748	End of the War of the Austrian Succession between Frederick the Great of Prussia and Maria Theresa of Austria	1898	Spanish-American War	1949	North Atlantic Treaty Organization Communists control China mainland Chiang Kaishek at Taiwan
		1899	Beginning of Boer War		
		1901	Marconi—first wireless message across the Atlantic		
1769	James Watt patented the steam engine	1903	Wright brothers flew in heavier-than-air machine at Kitty Hawk, North Carolina	1950	Korean War started
1770	Ludwig van Beethoven born: sonata and symphonic forms	1905	Einstein announced his Theory of Relativity End of Russo-Japanese War	1953	Mount Everest climbed by British expedition
1776	Declaration of American Independence	1909	Discovery of the North Pole by Peary	1954	United States Supreme Court decision against school segregation
1777	Battle of Saratoga	1911	Discovery of the South Pole by Amundsen	1957	Russian sputnik in orbit
1787	United States Constitution				
1789	French Revolution Washington first President of the United States	1912	Republic of China	1957–1958	International Geophysical Year
		1914	Beginning of World War I Battle of the Marne	1969	Americans landed on the moon
1804	Napoleon, Emperor of France				

(Page numbers in *italic* refer to illustrations.)

Abbott, Josephine L., 14
A Better Chance (ABC), 114
accreditation, 130–32
adding board, 42
Adler, Deirdre Spencer, 118
Advisory Council, 54, 55
Affleck, Grace Morris, 62
Allen, Bonnie, 85
Allen, Frederic W., 65
Alumnae Association, 47,
    62–63, 70, 82–83, 133, 139
Alumnae Bulletin, 82, 83, 87,
    109, 128
Alumnae Health Bureau, 63, *63*
Alumnae Luncheon, 83, *83,*
    109, *119,* 130, 139
Ames, Eleanor King, 24, 26,
    28–29, 41, 44, 47–49, *48*
Annenberg, Ambassador and
    Mrs. Walter H., 139, 144
Annenberg Center, *140,* 144, *145*
apprenticeships, 125
aprons, 21, *21*
Art Club, 127
art history, 120, 124
Arts Committee, 124–25
Athletic Association, 47–51, 54
Atterbury, Mrs. John, 12
Auchincloss, Priscilla Stanton,
    14–15, 42
Audubon Club, 39
Bailey, Margaret Emerson, *37,*
    37–38
Bailie, Earle, 65, 67
Bailie, Margaret Henderson, 9,
    27, 32, 69, 111
Barnes, Mrs. Courtlandt D., 65
Bartlett, Nancy, 121
Benik, Julia, *106*
Berendsen, Mildred Jeanmaire,
    9, 97, 102, *104,* 105–39, *109,*
    118, 122, 126, *131,* 136–39,
    141

Berendsen Room, 70, *120*
Bernkopf, Anna, 61
Bible verses, 41, 43, 54, 61
bird walks, *38,* 38–39
Bishop, Elsie, 71–72, *73*
Blagden, Lois, 103
Bloch, Hesse & Shalat, 121–22
Board of Trustees, 65, 75,
    76–77, 83–84, 100, 108–9,
    113, 130–32, 134, 136, 137,
    139, 141, 143, 149, 155
Bodden, Marlen, 113
Bodisch, Ann Rose, *106*
bookplate, *71*
Borock, Linda, 97, *97*–98,
    123–24
Bowie, W. Russell, 77
Brearley School, 12, 13, 15,
    83–84, 95, 125, 138, 139
Britton, Sandi Dinkins, 99
"Brownie Recipe," 70
Budget course, 35
bus service, 71, 88, 107, 109
Butler Rogers Baskett, 144
Buttrick, White & Burtis, 135
Career Day, 127, 133
Cartwright, Harriet, 17–18
Catherine, Saint, 18
Chapin-Brearley Exchange,
    83–84
Chapin, Maria Bowen, 7–77,
    8, 10, 12, 28, 30, 48, 76, 84,
    86, 111; death of, 76–77;
    outlook of, 17, 29, 55–57, 61,
    64, 68, 92–93, 144, 148
Chapin, Nicky Stout, 107
Chapin Chip, 126
Chapin School: birthday cele-
    brations for, 129–30, *130,*
    131; chronology of, 152–53;
    colors of, 47, 129; cur-
    riculum of, 17–18, 26–27,
    77, 89, 91, 93–95, 111–12,
    114, 124, 130–33; facilities
    of, 15, 16, 18, 21–25, *24,*
    65–71, *68, 110,* 111, *118, 118,*

120, *120*–22, *123,* 127, *134,*
    134–36, *135,* 144–46;
    founding of, 7–9, 15–16;
    incorporation of, 65, 77;
    motto of, 18; name change
    of, 76; philosophy of, 17, 29,
    55–57, 61, 64, 68, 79–80,
    92–93, 132–33, 143–44,
    148–49; faculty and staff of,
    31–41, 62, 71–74, 79, 93–95,
    129, 155; traditions of, 41–55;
    wheel as symbol of, 18
Cheska, Mary, 85, *85*
choir, 17, 26, 41
Choral Club, 95, 114, *131*
Christmas, 42, 43–45, *44, 131*
classics, 72, 74, 115
Club, The, 19, 45, 54, 75, 88, 108
Cog, The, 85
Colie, Elizabeth, 94, *94*
college admissions, 27, 125–26
coming-out parties, 62, 74
commencement, 9, 51–52, *52,*
    53, 76, 97, 116–18
community service, 89, 92, 115,
    125
computers, 120, 126, 146, *146*
Cox, Anne Finch, 42, 117
Crane, Jane Watson, 33
Croswell, James G., 12, 13, 15
Dance Club, 85
dates, 42, 156–57
Debating Club, 133–34
Delafield, J. Dennis, 134
Delano & Aldrich, 66, 69, 118
Demonstration Day, 50–51
Depression, Great, 74–75
Development Office, 130
diversity, 112–14, 130, 143–44,
    148, 149
dramatics, 40, 43, 44, 54, 62,
    84, 145–46
Drobney, Annie, *106*
Duer, Sophie, 55
Duloux, Marthe, 72, *73*
Early Steps, 114

East Harlem Protestant
    Parish, 113
Eaton, Marion, *2, 9*
Elliott, Osborn, 116–17
elocution, 17
Ely, Adele, 53
English, 37, 38, 112, 114, 124
Ethel Grey Stringfellow Art
    Case, 102
Faculty Show, 84, *84*
Fairfax, Mary Cecelia, 9, 16,
    18, 31–32, *32,* 42, 64–65, 69,
    70–76, 75–77, *86,* 146
February Week, 133
feminism, 91, 115, 127, 133
Field Day, *9,* 48, *49, 49,* 50, 75,
    75, 86, 95, *95*
field trips, 133
Fine Arts Club, 108
fire drills, 25
foreign languages, 61, 72, 124
Forensics Club, 133–34
Four Schools Placement
    Bureau, 84
fund drives, 67, 68, 82–84, 100,
    118, 120, 130, 134–35, 139, 144
Garfield, Jane Walker, 132
geography, 91, 112
Gildersleeve, Virginia C., 69,
    149
"God Our Father," 42
Gordon, Albert H., 120
Gordon, Polly Rousmaniere,
    118, 120
Gordon Room, 120, *130,* 144–45
Grandparents' Day, 133
Greek Festival, 49–50, *50*
greenhouse, 32, *33,* 69, 112,
    146, *147*
Gunderson, Joanna Bailie,
    8–9, 72
Harding, Charlotte, 15
Hasen, Charlotte Binger, 124
Havemeyer, Harry, 105, 117,
    137–38
Hedge, Audrey, 29

Henderson, Edward, 15, 23
Henderson, Louise, 114, 126, *126*
Herrick, Lois Hall, 19
Higgins, Jacqueline Holland, 113
history, 35–37, 89, 91, 105–6, 108, 112, 114, 126
Holland, Wanda, 113
Holt, Sylvia, 15
Hoppin, May Swords, 56
Hutter, Ruth, 112
Individual Study Program, 129
Interschool, 125
Irwin, Jane Darlington, 91
Iselin, Helen, 12, 15
Isham House, 19, *20*
Jackson, William E., 118
James, Louise Hoadley, 81, *82*
Janes, Mary L., 72–73, *73*, 112
Jennings, Frances, 79–80, *80*, 92–93, 98, 135
Johnson, Elizabeth Forrest, 77
Jones, Anne Keating, 80–81
Kendall, Anne, 40
Kerensky, Aleksandr, 108
kindergarten, 16, 121, 127, 146
Kinsolving, Arthur L., 102
Lawrence, Barbara Childs, 39
Lawrence, William, 68, 149
lecture series, 80, 102, 118
libraries, 70–71, *71*, *120*, 127, 144, *145*
life-skills program, 143, 144
Limelight, 42–43, 129
Lindbergh, Anne Morrow, 39, 52
Liu, Betty Wei, 36–37
Lloyd, Susan McIntosh, 80
Lloyd-Thomas, Nesta, 72, *73*, 74, 84, 93, *93*, 100, 115
lunch, 26, 69–70, 97, *111*, 127, 145
MacKenty, Katharine Walker, 32, 43, 47, 60, 83
Mahler, Lucy, 127
Manhattan Trade School for Girls, 21, 43, 44
Manning, William T., 76
Marlot School, 89–91
Mason, Katherine Post, 44

mathematics, 42, 72, 80, 112, 120, 124
Matthews, Doris, 60–61, *61*
McGregor, Ruth, 94, *94*
McIlvaine, Diana, 40
Mercer, Douglas D., *130*
Mestrovic, Jane, 126, *126*
Metherall, Isabel M., *73*, 74
Millikan, Robert, 69
Miss Abbott's School, 11, 14, 31, 64
Montessori, Maria, 64
moral development, 17, 29, 55, 59–60, 144
Morgan, Alma de Gersdorff, 51
Morgan, Maud Cabot, 22–23
Morison, Margaret, 38, *38*, 93
Morrow, Mrs. Dwight W., 65, 77
multiculturalism, 132–33, 143–44
mural, *127*, 127–28
music, 17–18, 91, 94–95, 114, 120, 124
Neale, Vivian, *114*, 115
Networking Evening, 133
News, 42, 61, 80, 89, 108, 127, 133
Nicoll, Alice, 88
Nightingale-Bamford School, 84, 95, 125
Olli, Corinne, 97, 98–99
"One Night When Stars Were Shining," 44
Paine, Patty Murphy, 143
Palmer, Julia Reed, 16
Parents' Association, 124–25
Pemberton, Catherine Watjen, 23, 25
penmanship, 17, 62, 73, 112
Pepukayi, 113
Perkins, Richard S., 100
Petas, Virginia, 130
Phelps, Judith, 114, *114*
physical education, 19, *20*, 25, 26, 39–40, 47–51, *48–50*, 58, 66, 71, 81, 95, *96*, 97–98, *98*, 123–24, 134, *135*, 145
Pierce, Elizabeth Gay, 31, 55
"Poem to Mildred Berensen," 138

Pope, Mary Barstow, 18, 22, 29, 32
posture, 40, 45, 84
Pound, 55
Powell, Lucy, 106, 107, 125–26
Pratt, Mrs. Harold I., 7, 65, 69
Prayers, 24, 25, 41, 42–43, *43*, 54, 61, 75, 76, 95, *122*, 123, *136*, 142, 148, *148*
Prep for Prep, 114
Primary Classes for Girls, 13–15, 16, 41
Proffitt, Ruth, 72–73, 135, *135*
public service officers, 55
public speaking, 42, 133
Rancoigne, Baroness de, 47
Rand, Adaline Havemeyer, 74
Rand, Ellen Emmett, *8*, 70, 77
Red Cross, 60–61, *60*, *61*, 88
Reed, Lansing P., 65
"Rhyme of the English Kings, The," 36–37
Robbins, Cera B., 130, 134, 138
Roberts, Mary Gordon, 144
Roger Ascham School, 19
Roosevelt, Franklin D., 87
Roosevelt, George Emlen, 65, 95
Savage, May Terry, 15
Scarborough School, 71, 95
Scholarship Foundation, 63–64
school song, *6*, 18
Schrade, Robert, *94*, 94–95, 114, *131*
Schwartz, Richard J., 135
science, 21, 25, 38–39, 94, 112, 121, 124, 127, 133, 135
Self-Government, 53–55, *54*, *55*, 88, 113, 115, *121*, 154
Semmes, Shelby H., 93–94, *94*
Shalat, Herbert, 121–22
Sheldon, Alethia, 11
spelling rules, 62
Spence, Clara B., 15, 57
Spence School, 69, 84, 125
Sprague, Dorothy Whitmarsh, 144
Stackelberg, Ellen Biddle, 41
Standard, Paul, 112
Stanton, Phoebe Rentschler, 132

Stewart, E. Grace, *38*, 38–39, 94
Strategic Goals for 1997–2007, 143–44
Stringfellow, Ethel Grey, 9, 25, 28, 32–35, *34*, 41, 44, 45, 52, 56, 57, 64, 69, 70, 75–76, *76*, 78, 79–103, *84*, *86*, *93*, *95*, *101*, 105–9, 111, 112, 117–19, *118*, *119*, 125–26
Stringfellow Library, *120*, 120–21
Stringfellow Wing, 118, 127
suffragettes, 56–57, *57*
summer activities, 52–53, 89
tea, 53, 97, 98, 108
Tenney, Margaret Brett, 61
Thanksgiving, 42–43, *43*, 148
Theunick, Sandra, 9, *139*, 141–49, *142*, 149
Trautman, Susanah Bailie, 85
uniforms, 21, *21*, 45–47, *45*, *46*, 54, 55, 81–82, *82*, 119, 125
Van Rensselaer, Georgina Wells, 55, 56, 62
Wagemann, Oscar, 80, 89
Walbridge, Elizabeth Mason, 32, 74, 124
Walker, Charles, 114, *114*
Walker, Roberts, 65
Ward, Jane Wyatt, 62
Warren, Ralph R., Jr., 119
Webb, Aileen Osborn, 19, 65, 67
Webster, Elizabeth Brett, 130
Wetmore, Alice, 12–15, 16
Wheel, The, 18, 19, 36, 51, 54, 55, *55*, 59–61, *60*, 70–71, 74, 76, 82, *82*, 85–87, 91, 128–29
Whiteside, Mary Norman, 99, *99*, 116
Wilde, Julia, 16, 40–41
Wilkinson, Katharine May, *35*, 35–37, 45, 49–50, 52, 54, 59, 67, 68, 89, 93, 105–6
Wilson, Woodrow, 57, 60
Woodbridge, Catherine, 97
World War I, 47, 60–61
World War II, 86–91, 95
Yates, Grace, *39*, 39–40, 45, 47, 84
Yorkville Youth Council, 92

The Chapin School admits students of any race, religion, color, sexual orientation, national and ethnic origin to all the rights, privileges, programs and activities generally accorded or made available to students at the school. It does not discriminate on the basis of race, religion, color, sexual orientation, national and ethnic origin in administration of its educational policies, admissions policies, scholarships and loan programs, and athletic and other school-administered programs.